'Uma

MAKERS OF ISLAMIC CIVILIZATION

This series, conceived by the Oxford Centre for Islamic Studies and jointly published by Oxford University Press and I.B.Tauris, provides an introduction to outstanding figures in the history of Islamic civilization. Written by leading scholars, these books are designed to be the essential first point of reference for any reader interested in the growth and development of Islamic history and culture.

General Editor: DR F. A. NIZAMI
Series Manager: R. M. RITTER

'Umar

Shibli Numani

An abridged edition of Shibli Numani's
'Umar al-Fārūq

Oxford Centre for Islamic Studies

I.B.TAURIS

LONDON · NEW YORK

Published in 2004 by I.B. Tauris & Co Ltd and Oxford University Press India
in association with the Oxford Centre for Islamic Studies

I.B. Tauris & Co Ltd
6 Salem Road, London W2 4BU
175 Fifth Avenue, New York NY 10010
www.ibtauris.com

In the United States of America and Canada distributed by
Palgrave Macmillan, a division of St. Martin's Press
175 Fifth Avenue, New York NY 10010

ISBN 1 85043 670 3
EAN 978 1 85043 670 6

For all territories except South Asia

A full CIP record for this book is available from the British Library
A full CIP record is available from the Library of Congress

Library of Congress Catalog Card Number: available

Typeset in GoudyOlst BT
by Eleven Arts, Keshav Puram, Delhi 110 035
Printed in India by Pauls Press, New Delhi 110 020

Contents

Contents

List of maps

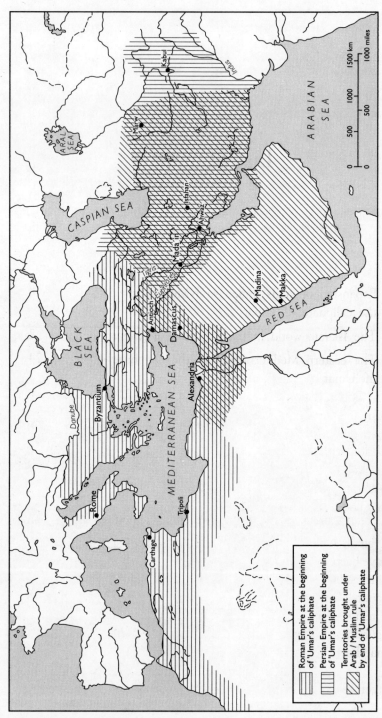

Map: 1. Expansion of lands under Arab/Muslim rule in the caliphate of 'Umar

ARABIAN
SEA

1500 km
1000
500
0

1000 miles
500
0

Kabul

Indus

Marw

ARAL
SEA

CASPIAN SEA

Isfahan

Ahwaz

Mada'in

Tigris

Euphrates

Madina

Makka

RED SEA

Antioch

Damascus

BLACK
SEA

Alexandria

Byzantium

Donube

MEDITERRANEAN SEA

Rome

Tripoli

Carthage

Roman Empire at the beginning
of 'Umar's caliphate

Persian Empire at the beginning
of 'Umar's caliphate

Territories brought under
Arab / Muslim rule
by end of 'Umar's caliphate

A Note on the Abridgement

The first, Urdu, edition of this study of the life of 'Umar by Mawlana Shibli Numani was published in India in 1898, after four years of research in many libraries including those of Berlin, Paris, and London. It straightaway won great acclaim as the best and most authoritative account of its subject. The book raced through several editions in Urdu, and was then translated into Turkish and Persian. The English translation by Mawlana Zafar Ali Khan was (though done much earlier) first published in 1939, again to such acclaim that, despite wartime shortages of paper, a revised two-volume edition was issued in 1943, then reprinted at four- or five-year intervals thereafter. This abridgement is based upon the 1975 reprint (Ashraf Press, Lahore), which is still available.

The two volumes of Zafar Ali Khan's translation run to about 650 pages. This abridgement retains therefore only a sixth of the original. The footnotes and extensive quotations from sources have been omitted outright. The narrative of the battles, the detail of the administrative reforms, and much of the anecdotal material about 'Umar, have been greatly condensed. So too, most of the 'direct speech', attributed either to 'Umar himself or to other major figures in the narrative, has been left out. For the few, short passages that have been retained, in an effort to reflect the literary (as distinct from scholarly) ambition of the Urdu original, sources are given where these could be traced—but they could not always be traced. The date and sequence of events as accepted by most Muslim historians, Shibli Numani included, is strongly contested by non-Muslim scholars. Here, as is only proper, we have followed the dating as given in the work being abridged, and in the Hijri form: without going into the kind of detailed discussion of the sources that would interest only specialists, the labour of calculating Common Era equivalents for Hijri dates that are disputed would have been pointless.

The principal aim and rationale of the abridgement was to produce, for the non-specialist, a short, readable essay that retained the central argument of Shibli Numani's comprehensive study. Before turning to explain why, a century after it was first put forward, that argument deserves to be made more widely known, a brief indication of some of the author's sources will be useful.

Shibli Numani's presentation of 'Umar's contribution to the evolution of Islamic law follows Shah Wali-Allah's treatise on the subject in *Izalat al-khafa'*, and he also draws upon the *Musannaf* of Ibn Abi Shayba. Otherwise, for the historical narrative proper, he indicates that he made most frequent reference, in addition to the well-known collections of Hadith, to sources such as the *Ma'arif* of Ibn Qutayba (d. 276/898); *Kitab al-akhbar al-tiwal* of Ahmad b. Da'wud Abu Hanifa Dinawari (d. 281/903); the *Tabaqat* of Ibn Sa'd; *Ta'rikh Ya'qubi* of Ibn Wadih al-'Abbasi (fl. 3rd century/ 9th century); *Futuh al-buldan* and *Ansab al-ashraf* of al-Baladhuri (d. 279/901); the *Ta'rikh* of al-Tabari (d. 310/932); *Kitab al-kharaj* of Qadi Abu Yusuf (d. 182/804); and the *Muruj al-dhahab* and *Kitab al-tanbih wa-l-ashraf* of al-Mas'udi (d. 386/1008).

In most cases, critical editions and evaluations of these materials were not available when Shibli Numani wrote his life of 'Umar: he read them either in manuscript or in printed copies not done to modern standards. While modern scholarship has made it possible for historians to read the traditional sources more sceptically and be more accurate about particular incidents, it has failed to give a better understanding of the achievements of 'Umar's life as a whole. What most challenges understanding is how feuding clans of largely nomadic tribesmen were able, in about ten years, to secure an enduring military conquest of almost all of the Persian empire and two major provinces of the Roman empire, namely Syria and Egypt. Explanations in the style of modern scholarship claim that the Arabs marched in a trance of religious fervour, or out of desperation for food and plunder, or some combination of the two, against the background of a terminal military weakness in the empires bordering the Arabian Peninsula. Even in major academic works on the subject, regarded as august and authoritative, for example the *Cambridge History of Iran* (vol. iv, 1975), we come across claims such as the following:

[The claim that Khalid was ordered by Abu Bakr] to invade Iran according to a concerted and carefully arranged plan would appear to be a romantic historical fiction . . . [Nevertheless] there is evidence that skirmishing was beginning to develop into more regular warfare . . . preliminary preparations had been made. (p. 7)

Not that religion was by any means the sole inspiration of the Arabs at the outset; it cannot be denied that poverty and hunger were powerful goads to action and avarice. The Prophet had promised that the treasures of the Chosroes and Caesars were destined for the Arabs . . . . The caliph also encouraged the Muslim community to jihad, especially as, since the suppression of the Ridda, the numbers of Muslims in Arabia and on its perimeters day by day increased. It was necessary to send them out to fresh lands, both for the sake of their stomachs and in order to restrain civil strife. (pp. 17–18)

Leaving aside the inconsistencies in this explanation (there was no plan to invade Iran, but the Prophet had promised its treasures), it fails because it does not tell us *how* raids were converted into a programme of conquest. The raiders would have needed to learn, and learn very quickly, how to coordinate their military operations, to stay in the field after a successful raid, to link the ambitions of individual clans into a coherent, sustained campaign, to find the motivation to settle in the territories conquered (that is, not go home with their booty), then govern those territories . . . and so on.

The merit of Shibli Numani's work is the explanatory effectiveness of its central argument. His account links the military conquests, which defined for good Islam's geographical heartlands, with the reforms 'Umar achieved in law, government, and administration, which defined many of Islam's important characteristics as a civilization. The Arabs earned unprecedented success on the battlefield by superior morale and superior command, both directly inspired by the ideal of a just social order, an Islamic polity, as represented in the personal character and style of government of the Caliph. The conquests succeeded, that is, they endured, because the elite who led the campaigns and administered the conquered peoples and territories believed in the integrity of 'Umar as a Muslim ruler. His insight and competence in understanding the Qur'an and the Prophet's teaching gave to his exercise of power an almost irresistibly persuasive authority. By his own example, as well as through specific administrative measures, he replaced loyalty to clan with loyalty to Islam, thereby unifying the Arabs in a universal order which easily embraced non-Arabs and non-Muslims. Without that higher loyalty, it is inconceivable that the Muslims could have even held on to, let alone greatly expanded, their territorial gains, after the assassination of 'Umar.

This abridgement will have been worthwhile to the extent that, while removing much else of Shibli Numani's original, it conveys clearly this core of its argument.

Jamil Qureshi

Oxford
June 2004

Part I

The Conquests

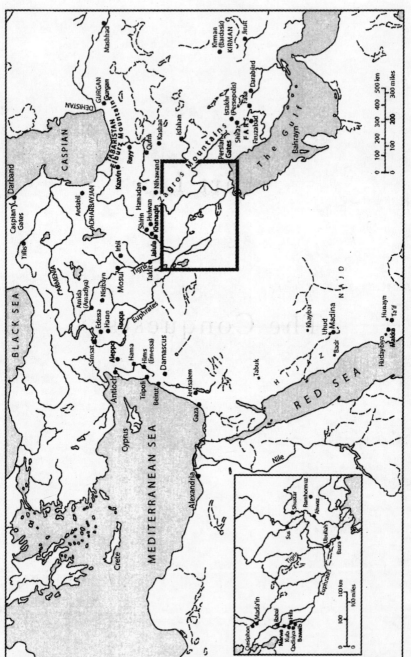

Map. 2. The Islamic world in the caliphate of 'Umar

1

'Umar's Accession to the Caliphate

Early life and training

Little is known for certain about 'Umar's life before his conversion to Islam. However, we can be sure that at least some of his great qualities—notably, his sense of personal authority, his daring and physical strength, and his political acumen—derived from his family background and early training. 'Umar was a 'born leader', a direct descendant of 'Adiy, chief of one of the ten clans of the wealthiest and most prestigious tribe in Arabia, the Quraysh. 'Adiy was the principal negotiator for the Quraysh in any inter-clan or inter-tribal dispute. Among those of his descendants who held the same office, 'Umar's grandfather, Nufayl b. 'Abd al-'Uzza, was specially renowned. He arbitrated a dispute over leadership of the tribe between 'Abd al-Muttalib and Harb b. 'Ummayya in favour of the former, the grandfather of the future Prophet.

The pre-eminence of the Quraysh over the other tribes of the Arabian Peninsula rested largely upon their role as guardians of the Ka'ba, the holy shrine in Makka. Since this shrine was dedicated to the worship of idols, the authority of 'Umar's family was vested in preserving that worship. It is remarkable, therefore, that 'Umar's cousin, Zayd, also a grandson of the famous Nufayl, should have been an ardent monotheist who preached a return to the religion of Abraham, traditionally recognized (and confirmed by the Qur'an) as the founder of the Ka'ba. Persecuted by his own family, Zayd was finally driven from the city. Some say he took refuge in the mountain caves of Hira where, years later, the revelation of the Qur'an began. The most zealous of Zayd's persecutors was his uncle, 'Umar's father, Khattab.

Khattab's dedication to the pagan values of the Quraysh is clear from his severity with 'Umar. It was normal for Makkan nobles to send their sons out to the desert to pasture camels, and 'Umar endured this disciplining in Dajnan, a plain about ten miles from Qudayd near Makka. When, long afterwards, as Caliph, 'Umar passed by Dajnan, he glorified God and commented: 'There was a time when I roamed this desert as a camel-herd, dressed in a felt jacket, and whenever I sat down tired, my father would beat me. Now I live a time when I need reckon none as my superior save God' (Ibn Sa'd, 3:266–7).

'Umar is known to have taken part in wrestling and equestrian competitions in the fair held each year at 'Ukaz, near the 'Arafat hills—he can hardly have done so if he did not excel in these sports. Expert knowledge of the genealogy of the Arab tribes 'Umar inherited from his father and grandfather. He was, again like them, a formidable negotiator and public speaker: he served the Quraysh in the role of ambassador before his conversion to Islam made him their enemy. Also before that event, 'Umar had developed a sophisticated ear for the poetry in which the Arab peoples took such pride, and had memorized the best of it. Poetry at that time was largely an oral performance but, exceptionally among his contemporaries, 'Umar had learnt to read and write.

'Umar's breadth of mind and capacity to understand and assimilate the ways of other peoples, a feature of his rule as Caliph, may have developed during his extensive and frequent journeys out of Arabia into Syria and Persia. He travelled for business but was always keen to meet the distinguished persons in the places where he stayed. Sadly, detailed accounts of 'Umar's travels, once extant, have long since disappeared. We know for certain only that he travelled much and was a successful trader.

'Umar's conversion to Islam

By the time Islam began to be preached among the Quraysh, 'Umar, then about twenty-seven years old, was already a public figure highly esteemed by his peers among the Quraysh. However, in opposition to the tide of Islam, all his virtues worked against themselves—his sense of honour was expressed as arrogant tribal pride, his power of conviction as narrow-minded stubbornness, his physical courage as determined lack of feeling. Conversely, once he moved with the tide of Islam, all of his qualities found the sufficient reason (and the scope) to grow into their true and full forms.

Just as his father had persecuted Zayd, 'Umar persecuted converts to Islam with a violent ardour. Zayd's son, Sa'id, was among the first to become Muslim and his wife Fatima, 'Umar's sister, converted also. Neither revealed their conversion to 'Umar. Labina, a female slave in 'Umar's household, failed to conceal her conversion from him and he beat her harshly on many occasions in a vain effort to make her recant. He also failed to beat the faith out of others.

In frustration 'Umar made up his mind to kill the Prophet, buckled on his sword for the purpose and set out. On the way he met with a fellow clansman, Nu'aym b. 'Abdullah, another secret convert. When Nu'aym realized 'Umar's intention, he diverted him by advising that he deal first with his own near family, his sister and brother-in-law. Enraged at this news, 'Umar turned back to his sister's house. She had been reciting passages of the Qur'an but stopped on hearing 'Umar approach. He asked her what she had been reciting. When she tried to evade telling him, he accused her and her husband of heresy. He then set upon his brother-in-law, Sa'id. Fatima tried to intervene but 'Umar struck her with such force she bled. She then said: ''Umar, do whatever you will, Islam cannot be forced from our hearts.'

Those words and the sight of his sister bleeding stilled his anger. He asked to see what she had been reciting. His sister provided the fragment of writing she had hidden. He read from it words whose meaning is: 'Whatever is in the heavens or the earth glorifies God, the powerful, the wise' (57.1–7). Not for the first or last time, an admirer of Arabic poetry was overwhelmed by the literary miracle of the Qur'an. On reaching the words 'Believe in God and His Messenger', 'Umar uttered the creed: 'I believe that there is no god but God and that Muhammad is His Messenger.'

'Umar made his way to the house of Arqam, at the foot of the Safa hills, the meeting-place of the Muslims at that time and the Prophet's refuge. 'Umar was still wearing his sword. When the Prophet asked him the reason for his visit, 'Umar said simply: 'I come to embrace Islam.' The Prophet responded with *Allahu akbar* ('God is greater') and the assembly of Muslims repeated the cry. This event took place in the sixth year after the Revelation began (Baladhuri, *Ansab*, 5:346–50; Ibn Sa'd, 3:267–9; Ibn Athir, *Usd* 4:54–5; *Kamil*, 2:84–6).

'Umar's conversion was a grave loss to the Quraysh. He was now as militant on behalf of Islam as he had been against it. He argued for the Muslims' right to worship at the Ka'ba, a right hitherto denied them. His courage and persuasive skills defeated the vindictiveness of the Quraysh on this point—'Umar's first public triumph as a Muslim.

Emigration to Madina

The guardians of the Ka'ba, the Quraysh, could not foresee that the victory of Islam would make their shrine the greatest centre of pilgrimage in the world. Therefore, as more of their own number converted to Islam, their enmity intensified. They cruelly perse-cuted those Muslims who had no association of kinsfolk to defend them, and maintained a six-year economic and social boycott against all the Muslims together. In consequence, the Muslims' public worship was most severely constrained, and the social, economic, and legal dimensions of a full Muslim life could hardly evolve at all in Makka. However, the numbers of Muslims inside Makka continued to grow and, precisely because the Ka'ba was a focus of pilgrimage, so too did the numbers outside of Makka.

From Yathrib, an oasis township some 265 miles north of Makka, a substantial number of believers came to pledge their allegiance to the Prophet, and offered, under his leadership, to support and protect the Muslim community. The Prophet then ordered the Muslims to abandon their homes in Makka and settle in Yathrib. The great Emigration or *Hijra* began. 'Umar was among the earliest Emigrants, travelling in a group of about twenty including several of his own close relatives. As accommodation was not available in Yathrib, 'Umar settled initially a few miles away in the village of Quba'.

The Prophet himself made the Hijra, in the company of Abu Bakr, in the year 632, the thirteenth year after the Revelation began. He too stayed for a time in Quba'. Soon after arrival in Yathrib—subsequently known as the City of Light, Madina al-Munawwara—the Prophet concluded a treaty with all the tribes in the township, including the prosperous Jewish tribes who dominated its commercial life, pledging them to mutual defence and cooperation under his overall authority. He also arranged formal ties of brotherhood between the Emigrants (*Muhajirun*) from Makka and the Muslims of Madina. The latter, called the Helpers (*Ansar*), shared their wealth and property with their brothers-in-faith and generally took responsibility for their welfare. 'Umar's Ansari brother was 'Utban b. Malik, the chieftain of the Banu Salim. While 'Umar continued to live in Quba', he could not attend on the Prophet every day. He made an arrangement with 'Utban whereby each would be in Madina on alternate days and report to the other what he had heard from the Prophet.

The adhan *or call to prayer*

As the Muslims at last enjoyed some measure of security, it was possible to develop the institutions of worship denied them in Makka. The obligatory prayers of each day, congregational prayers on Fridays, fasting in the month of Ramadan followed by the

'Id al-fitr festival, and zakah (the alms tax), could now be regularly and fully observed. The method of summoning believers to prayer remained to be decided. Many of the Prophet's Companions favoured the use of some musical instrument, the practice of the Jews and Christians. While the matter was still under discussion, 'Umar suggested appointing a man to call people out. The Prophet accepted this suggestion straightaway and appointed Bilal as the first mu'adhdhin. It indicates how profoundly 'Umar was attuned to Islam that he had such a decisive part in the institution of the adhan or call to prayer: to this day, no other element of Muslim public life so clearly signals or characterizes a place as belonging to Islam.

After the Hijra

From the Hijra onward, 'Umar was actively involved in every significant development in the formative period of Islam until revelation of the Qur'an ended and the religion in its great essentials was complete. No battle was fought, no treaty negotiated, no administrative measure put in place, without 'Umar being consulted and his advice influencing the outcome. Even so, the major events of this period, their meaning and rationale, belong in a study that must make the Prophet's life its focus, not the life of his Companion, 'Umar. Here we can only review a few key incidents from the years 1–11 AH (i.e. after the Hijra). For a full, connected narrative, the reader should consult detailed biographies of the Prophet.

The battle of Badr

In the month of Ramadan, 2 AH, the Quraysh sent out a force of 950 armed men and cavalry in order to protect a returning trade caravan of theirs due to pass near Madina. The caravan of about forty men was led by Abu Sufyan. The Prophet urged the Muslims to go out and face the armed threat. As the Qur'an

(8.5–7) records, some Muslims, awed by the imbalance of the opposing forces and fearful of death, were reluctant to leave Madina, and some were keener to attack the caravan:

When your Lord caused you to leave your safe abode [Madina], a faction of the believers were averse to the action. They quarrelled with you about the truth after it was brought to light, thinking they were facing death and being driven to it. And whereas God promised you victory over one of the two hosts, [some among] you desired to get the upper hand over the undefended host [i.e. the caravan].

Battle was joined at Badr, some eighty miles from Madina. Out of 313 Muslims who took part, 83 were Emigrants (Muhajirun) and the rest Ansar. Out of the Emigrants, no less than twelve were from 'Umar's clan, the Banu 'Adiy. And, no doubt, it was out of respect for 'Umar that Banu 'Adiy were the only clan of Quraysh *not* represented on the enemy side. 'Umar fought at the Prophet's right hand throughout the affray, his freedman, Mihja', being the first Muslim killed. 'Umar faced and slew his maternal uncle, A'si b. Hisham b. Mughira. As we shall have occasion to record again, neither on this battlefield, nor upon any other, nor in any affair of government and administration, did family attachment ever take precedence over 'Umar's duty to Islam.

The Quraysh were utterly routed. Fourteen Muslims were killed at Badr. On the Quraysh side seventy were killed, including several nobles, and a similar number were taken prisoner. Among the prisoners too, there were eminent Quraysh nobles, such as 'Abbas, and 'Aqil the brother of 'Ali. When consulted by the Prophet, Abu Bakr advised that, as the prisoners were kinsfolk, they should be released against ransom. 'Umar advised that they should be beheaded and the execution carried out by each prisoner's Muslim relative. The Prophet followed the counsel of Abu Bakr. The following Qur'anic verse (8.67) may allude to this occasion: 'It is not [fitting] for a Prophet to hold captives until he has made slaughter in the land. You desire the attractions of the world and God desires [for you] the Hereafter.'

The battle of Uhud

Several of the Jewish clans in Madina, despite their treaty of mutual
defence with the Prophet, sent secret embassies to the Quraysh
to coordinate action against the Muslims. The Quraysh scarcely
needed incitement: they were determined on revenge for their
recent humiliation. The death of Abu Jahl at Badr left Abu Sufyan
as the chief instigator of war against the Muslims. Within a little
over twelve months he was able to send out a well-armed force
of 3,000. In the month of Shawwal, 3 AH, this army positioned
itself in two flanks below Mount Uhud, three miles out of Madina,
where they confronted a Muslim force of 700. Again the Quraysh
were out-fought and began to retreat with the vanguard of the
Muslims in pursuit. Victory was within the Muslims' grasp. However,
as they passed through the enemy camp, some of the Muslims
laid aside their weapons to secure spoils. Archers stationed by the
Prophet to defend against any cavalry attack from behind the
Muslims' main position deserted their posts to do the same. Seeing
this opening, the commander of the Quraysh second flank, Khalid
b. al-Walid, led a swift charge from behind. The Muslims were
ill-prepared to withstand the attack and scattered in disorder.
The Prophet himself was wounded, suffering injuries to his head
and face. He fell and was briefly hidden from sight. The cry arose
that he had been slain.

Some Muslims ran from the battlefield. Others stayed and
fought on, not caring to survive the Prophet. Still others stayed
on the field, but in a state of such shock at the enormity of their
loss that they could make no effort even to defend themselves.
'Umar was among those who suffered the extreme of shock. One
narrative of these moments in the battle is attributed to 'Umar
himself. 'Umar says that Anas b. Nadar approached him and asked
how it was with the Prophet. 'Umar answered that he thought
the Prophet was slain. Then Anas said it was his duty to God to
continue fighting and God was living still and watching him; then
he, Anas, fought on against the unbelievers until he was killed.

'Umar and Abu Bakr were among the first to race to the
Prophet when he rose and called his Companions. They formed

a defensive wall about him. The Muslim forces generally rallied and, fighting with an even greater commitment than before, drove the unbelievers back until they quit the field.

At Uhud the skill and presence of mind of Khalid b. al-Walid almost won a battle that had been lost for the Quraysh. Though neither side could claim actual victory, and though the losses of the Muslims were far more numerous, with many great men (including Hamza, the Prophet's uncle) slain, the moral triumph belonged to them. The Quraysh had failed to contain, still less reverse, the growing power of the Muslim community. And in a very short time indeed the military skills of Khalid b. al-Walid would be in the service of Islam, not against it.

Expulsion of the Banu Nadir

In 4 AH, 'Umar accompanied the Prophet and Abu Bakr to the settlements of the Jewish clan, the Banu Nadir, to ask for a loan, needed to pay compensation due from two Muslims for whom the Prophet took responsibility. By the terms of their treaty with the Muslims, the Banu Nadir were bound to assist the Muslims. Not only did they not do so, they attempted, during this mission, to have the Prophet assassinated. They were forthwith ordered to leave the city, taking all their movable wealth with them except arms and armour. The Banu Nadir at first resisted the order. However, after a brief siege while they waited in vain for help from other Jews and the Quraysh, they complied. Many settled in Khaybar, where they also held extensive lands. From there, their nobles openly sent emissaries to the Quraysh and other tribes across the Peninsula to persuade them to make a joint (and final) attack on the Muslims. An army of 10,000 was assembled and put under the command of Abu Sufyan, who marched once more on Madina in Shawwal of the following year (5 AH).

The battle of Khandaq (the Trench)

The Prophet did not go out to engage this large army. Instead, he elected to defend Madina from within. He ordered a wide

trench to be dug around the city, positioning distinguished
Companions at various points along the lines to prevent any breach.
This tactic, used for the first time in Arab warfare, wholly baffled
the attackers. They maintained a siege and blockade against the
city for a full month, attempting now and then to cross the trench.
The position along the trench for which 'Umar was responsible
is now marked by a mosque bearing his name.

The morale of the besiegers was gradually worn down. In single
combat, their champions were invariably beaten; the lines of defence
they faced seemed impregnable; and their Jewish allies within the
city proved untrustworthy, failing to come to their aid. In fact,
Nu'aym b. Mas'ud, one of their trusted emissaries, having secretly
converted to Islam, had very skilfully created mistrust between
the Jews and the Quraysh. In the end, having achieved nothing
at all, the Quraysh and their Arab allies had little choice but
to withdraw.

The truce of Hudaybiya

Towards the end of Shawwal in the following year, the Prophet
set out for Makka with about 1,400 Muslims, intending pilgrimage.
As they neared Makka, they learnt that, contrary to established
custom, the Quraysh were resolved to prevent the entry of the
Muslim pilgrims. Taking a roundabout route, therefore, the Muslims
halted just outside the city boundary at Hudaybiya. The Prophet
asked 'Umar to go and negotiate the rights due to them from
the guardians of the Ka'ba. 'Umar pointed out that the Quraysh
were his bitter enemies and that there were none of his clan present
in Makka to support him. At his suggestion, 'Uthman, several
of whose relatives and friends were in Makka, was deputed instead.

Some days passed without the return of 'Uthman. The Muslims
had to presume that the Quraysh had killed him. The Prophet
made all the Muslims individually take an oath of allegiance by
which they vowed to fight the unbelievers. 'Umar was already
arming himself when he learnt of this and hastened to the Prophet
to make his pledge.

This demonstration of absolute resolve must have inclined the Quraysh to reflect and, after reflection, to negotiate. The negotiations were both tense and protracted. Their outcome was a ten-year truce between the two parties.

According to the terms of Hudaybiya, normal contacts between the Muslims and the Quraysh and their respective allies were henceforth permitted and acts of war prohibited. However, the Muslims had to turn back from Makka, not being permitted to make the pilgrimage until the following year. Also, during the period of the truce, any associate of Quraysh who defected to the Muslim side must be returned to them, but any Muslim who defected to the Quraysh would not be returned. The apparent inequity of this arrangement incensed 'Umar, who felt that the Muslim side had been slighted. He discussed his feelings with Abu Bakr, who assured him that whatever the Prophet decided must be for the best. He then took his reservations directly to the Prophet:

'O Prophet of God, are you not the Messenger of God?'
'Without doubt I am.'
'Are not our enemies idol-worshipping polytheists?'
'Without doubt they are.'
'Why then should we suffer our religion to be humiliated?'
'I am God's Messenger and I do not act in contravention of His commands.'

(Ibn Hisham, 3:331)

'Umar cannot have imagined that any convert to Islam would return to unbelief if returned to the Quraysh. What troubled him, knowing well the arrogance of the idolaters, was that they could present the terms of Hudaybiya as a victory over Islam. He repented for the rest of his life that he had questioned the judgement of the Prophet and strove to expiate the sin by prayers and fasting, alms-giving and emancipating slaves. On the way back to Madina, the Prophet received revelation of sura al-Fath (Victory) and recited its verses to 'Umar and so eased his heart: 'We have opened wide for you the gates of victory. . .' (48.1) (Ibn Hajar, 7:560).

The renewal of normal contacts between the Muslims and the unbelievers provided, for the first time, an opportunity to present

Islam in practice as well as precept, and without the background of belligerence: more people accepted the faith in the next two years than had accepted it in the previous eighteen.

The battle of Khaybar

The terms of the truce did not embrace all the Arab tribes, and the same Jews who had instigated the failed battle of the Trench sought and found other allies than the Quraysh. In 6 AH they persuaded the Banu Sa'd to make war on the Muslims: this effort, too, failed. The Jews then allied with the clans of Ghatafan, whom they urged to the battlefield while themselves preparing war from behind the substantial towers and fortifications of their strongholds around Khaybar.

In 7 AH, the Prophet led out a force of 1,600 against Khaybar. Abu Bakr and 'Umar on separate occasions commanded valiant but unsuccessful assaults on the fortifications. A breach, and decisive victory, were finally achieved by 'Ali. The Prophet distributed the lands of Khaybar among those who had fought in the battle. 'Umar set aside his share as a *waqf* or charitable endowment—the first such endowment in Islamic history.

The conquest of Makka

Two feuding tribes, Khuza'a and Bakr, had stopped fighting under the terms of Hudaybiya. In the year 8 AH, the Banu Bakr, allies of the Quraysh, re-opened hostilities. The Quraysh abetted them in their war to the extent of even harrying Khuza'a refugees who sought sanctuary in the precincts of the Ka'ba. Since the Banu Khuza'a were under the protection of the Muslims, the Quraysh realized that they had broken the terms of Hudaybiya. Abu Sufyan travelled in person to Madina to plead with the Prophet to renew the treaty. The Prophet listened to him but made no answer. Abu Sufyan then appealed to others including Abu Bakr and 'Umar. The latter cut his plea short with stern implacability.

The Prophet made swift preparations to march on Makka.

He set out in Ramadan at the head of a force of 10,000, making a halt a little way from the city. 'Abbas, who had been sent on ahead to offer terms, met with Abu Sufyan and persuaded him to accompany him back to the Prophet where he, 'Abbas, would plead for him. 'Umar saw the two approach and, guessing 'Abbas' purpose, asked the Prophet's leave to 'behead this enemy who has after so long fallen into our hands' (Ibn Hisham, 4:45). But the Prophet granted Abu Sufyan his life, entered Makka unopposed and extended amnesty to all his former enemies. Inside Makka, he climbed the mount of Safa and delivered a magnificent, moving speech that enabled bitter enemies to become reconciled to each other within the embrace of Islam. The people came in throngs to swear allegiance to him. The idols in the Ka'ba were destroyed.

The battle of Hunayn

The Hawazin were a numerous and wealthy tribe, settled mostly to the east and south of Makka. They were related and allied to the Thaqif, who were the guardians of the shrine to the goddess al-Lat in the fertile and temperate city of Ta'if. The woman who had been a foster-mother to the Prophet when he was an infant came from a sub-clan of Hawazin, the Banu Sa'd b. Bakr. In spite of this connection, all the clans of Hawazin were hostile to Islam and observed the Muslims' growing strength with jealous alarm. Perhaps because they mistakenly supposed that the Muslims' march south from Madina was directed at them, perhaps for some other motive, the Hawazin had assembled a large, offensive force even before the conquest of Makka. The willingness with which about 2,000 Makkans joined the 10,000-strong Muslim force implies that they saw the Hawazin preparations as an opportunistic venture to take Makka.

The Muslims marched southwards from Makka to face the Hawazin who awaited them in the valley of Hunayn and in the ravines bordering it. After initial success when, once again, some Muslims were distracted into gathering spoils, the Muslims were caught in a well-prepared ambush and caused to retreat in considerable disorder, suffering heavy losses. 'Umar was prominent among the Emigrants who remained steadfast beside the Prophet, as did the Prophet's Makkan kinsmen, Abu Sufyan among them, so recently his bitter enemies. Eventually, the sheer authority of the Prophet's being among the Muslims rallied them and they fought back vigorously. A defeat was, quite incredibly, turned into a victory. The Qur'an (9.25–6) refers explicitly to this battle:

God has given you victory on many fields and on the day of Hunayn when you exulted in your great numbers but they were of no avail to you and the earth, though so spacious, was made narrow for you, and you turned back in flight! Then God sent down His peace upon His Messenger and upon the believers, and sent down hosts you could not see, and punished the unbelievers.

In terms of scale, this was certainly the Muslims' greatest victory so far—as many as 6,000 prisoners were taken.

Following a brief campaign against Ta'if, the Prophet returned to Madina: he had promised the Ansar that Madina was to be his city, not (as they feared) Makka.

Epistles; battle of Mu'ta; expedition to Tabuk

In the year 6 AH, the Prophet had conveyed to neighbouring rulers and kings written letters inviting them to accept Islam. His emissary to the Persian court was treated with great arrogance. The Persian Emperor regarded all Arabs as his vassals. Outraged at being offered advice by 'a slave', he tore up the Prophet's letter and issued an order to his governor in Yemen that the Prophet should be arrested and brought to the imperial court. However, shortly thereafter, the Emperor was murdered by his son and no attempt was made to carry out this threat.

The Prophet's emissary to Heraclius, the Roman emperor, was waylaid, abused, and robbed on his return journey, in the territory of the Syrian Arab tribe Jadham. The emissary to the territory of Basra was also put to death. In all, some fifteen of the Prophet's emissaries were killed by tribesmen belonging to the Ghassan tribe or their associates and allied clans. To check these abuses, the Prophet in 8 AH sent out an army of about 3,000 against them, no doubt aware that they could at any time call on the armies of their patrons, the Romans. On the march, the Muslims became aware that the Arabs had indeed been reinforced in strength by regular troops of the Roman army. Nevertheless, they pressed on towards the Dead Sea, where, against overwhelming odds, they faced annihilation. Three of the closest and most distinguished of the Prophet's Companions were slain: Zayd b. Harith, Ja'far Tayyar and 'Abdullah b. Rawaha. When command passed to Khalid b. al-Walid, now a believer, the Muslims were able to organize and effect a retreat with few further losses. After this, the battle of Mu'ta, Khalid was honoured with the title 'Sword of God'.

The threat from the Ghassanis and their allies persisted. Indeed, a rumour spread among the Muslims that the Roman emperor, following successful campaigns against the Persians in Syria and Palestine, was preparing an invasion of Arabia. The Muslims had witnessed at Mu'ta the organization and depth of power in men and equipment of the Roman forces. The Prophet urged the believers to provide and equip an army capable of responding to this danger. Most of the Companions who had means contributed large sums of money, 'Umar donating no less than half of all his wealth. In 9 AH, the Prophet marched the Muslims out at great speed in the hottest season of the year. At Tabuk, they awaited the Roman invasion: it never came—possibly the Romans had been deterred by the demonstration of resolve and discipline, or the rumour of invasion had been ill-founded.

The Prophet's farewell pilgrimage

In the following year (10 AH), the Prophet received deputations from all parts of Arabia and people embraced Islam in their thousands. Also in this year, the Prophet made his last pilgrimage to the House of God in Makka. For the first time in centuries, only God was worshipped at this shrine, according to the tradition of Abraham. During the rites at 'Arafat, the Prophet delivered his last sermon, urging the Muslims to unity, equality, and brotherhood, to hold fast to the Qur'an and his example, and to secure each other's rights.

The Prophet's illness and death

The Prophet completed preparations for a military expedition against the Romans in the month of Safar, 11 AH, and appointed the very young Usama, son of Zayd b. Harith who was killed at Mu'ta, to command it. However, this expedition had to be postponed when the Prophet fell ill. He suffered an intense but intermittent fever. Sometimes he was too unwell to attend prayers in the mosque—he indicated that Abu Bakr was to take his place and lead the worshippers. At other times, including the very morning of his death, he was well enough to watch the people at prayer— his profound contentment at this sight was reflected in his face.

The Prophet's illness lasted some thirteen days in all, during which time, when well enough, he was often able to summon his close Companions to console and counsel them. Only two days before his death, he had recovered sufficiently for Abu Bakr to return to his home, two miles from Madina. 'Umar was near the Prophet up to his last moments.

The Prophet died at about midday on Monday, 12 Rabi' I, in the apartment of his beloved wife, 'A'isha. He was buried in the same place a little after noon on the next day.

The most widely accepted tradition is that 'Umar could not bear, and therefore would not believe, news of the Prophet's death. He is reported to have gone to the Mosque and threatened to slay anyone who said that the Prophet was dead.

'Umar will have understood better than most what the implications of the event were. It meant that the Muslims must now carry the responsibilities of Islam without the support of direct Divine guidance if a new situation arose, and a new situation would arise. It meant that, in a rapidly expanding community, unity and equity and justice must somehow be maintained between individuals and tribes without the arbitration of a man whose judgement was informed and supported from the Unseen. Bearing in mind also 'Umar's moments of near paralysis at Uhud and given that his intense love for the Prophet might not, for a few moments at least, allow him to endure the certainty of separation, it is possible that he did make such a threat.

Another way to construe what 'Umar is reported to have said is not to regard it as an outburst but as a warning, from one whose opinion carried great weight. 'Umar may have feared that those whose allegiance to Islam was shallow or even false could use the occasion of public disquiet and uncertainty to create disorder. Therefore, he forbade the news to be carelessly publicized until the question of where overall authority now rested had been settled.

The question of the succession

The potential for disorder and disunity was considerable. The issue of who was to carry the responsibility for the future of Islam and the Muslim community was urgent. While there were, no doubt, many individuals who might have desired power for its own sake, those who could be believed to seek that responsibility in order to serve Islam fell into three groups. There were, first, the Emigrants, of whom the most senior figures were Abu Bakr and 'Umar, and who could command the allegiance of the Quraysh tribe as a whole; second, the Ansar, the Muslims of Madina, who had supported the Prophet's mission from before the battle of Badr and whose spokesman was Sa'd b. Ubada, the chief of the Banu Sa'ida; third, the Banu Hashim, the Prophet's own clan, led by 'Ali, who was respected for his piety as well as his heroism on the battlefield and who enjoyed the distinction of being the father of the Prophet's beloved grandsons, Hasan and Husayn.

It could not be expected from the senior figures of any of these groups that they should indulge in personal lamentations for the Prophet when the future of the mission to which the Prophet had devoted his life might be jeopardized by their doing so. What is troubling is that any of them should have reflected upon the discharge of their responsibility separately from the others. Even before the Prophet's body had been buried, the Ansar gathered in the meeting-place of the Banu Sa'ida, and Zubayr, 'Abbas and others who supported Banu Hashim met with 'Ali in the house of his wife, Fatima, the Prophet's daughter.

Different narratives of the events in the traditions give different perspectives, further complicated by looking back upon those narratives through the troubled history that followed them. Here, it is only fitting to give special place to the perspective of 'Umar, insofar as records of it are available.

Abu Bakr hastened, as soon as the news reached him, to the apartment of his daughter 'A'isha. 'Umar was already there or was admitted subsequently. According to the account in the *Musnad* of Abu Ya'la, a man called from outside asking 'Umar to come to him. 'Umar asked to be left in peace as they were busy in making arrangements for the Prophet's funeral. On the man's insistence 'Umar did go out and learnt that the Ansar were gathering in force at the hall of the Banu Sa'ida. Lest the Ansar should do something that might lead to war, 'Umar persuaded Abu Bakr to accompany him to their gathering. Other senior Emigrants also attended (Ibn Hajar, 7:36).

There, they duly acknowledged the very great sacrifices that the Ansar had made for the cause of Islam but explained also that there were now many and diverse Arab tribes who had embraced Islam and who, for generations past, had not accepted the pre-eminence of any tribe except the Quraysh. Likewise, the Quraysh as a whole would not suffer to be led by anyone from the Ansari tribes. Thus, if the Ansar claimed to succeed to the authority of the Prophet there was bound to be disunity. 'Umar then praised Abu Bakr, whom the Prophet himself had chosen to accompany him in his Emigration from Makka and whom he had appointed to lead them all in prayer. Who would consent to pray behind any other person if Abu Bakr was one of the assembly? Finally, 'Umar put his hand in the hand of Abu Bakr and swore allegiance to him, other senior Emigrants followed his example and then the Ansar likewise.

The narrative of these events as recorded in Bukhari, where

it is attributed to 'Umar himself, very particularly notes the threat of political factionalism at this time, with the Ansar and 'Ali, Zubayr and their followers forming two distinct groups so that, thereafter, the Emigrants formed a third (Bukhari, 8:541).

Though 'Ali was profoundly saddened by the way that the election of Abu Bakr had been presented to him, namely as a *fait accompli*, eventually he too was reconciled to it. Following his decision to accept Abu Bakr, others of the Banu Hashim and their supporters acquiesced also. For the time at least, 'Umar's forceful and decisive conduct had prevented discord.

Abu Bakr and the succession of 'Umar

The rule of Abu Bakr lasted just two years and three months (10–12 AH). These years were marked by campaigns against apostates and false 'prophets', and the launch of expeditions, as intended by the Prophet before his death, in the direction of Iraq and Syria.

Abu Bakr was certain in his own mind that he wished 'Umar to succeed him. However, he consulted with senior figures before making his choice known. No one doubted that 'Umar was the most able man for the task. However, several of those consulted expressed the reservation that 'Umar's severity of temperament might cause conflict. Abu Bakr argued that the perceived severity of 'Umar was a proper counterbalance to the perceived gentleness of his own style, and that, once in office, they would find 'Umar's manner much changed. A document of testament was duly prepared and read out in public. Abu Bakr then asked the assembly if they accepted his nomination of 'Umar. They did.

Abu Bakr died in the month of Jumada II in 13 AH. Before his death, he called 'Umar to him and offered him much impressive and valuable advice to serve him in the discharge of his responsibilities as Caliph. At one time one of the chief persecutors of the believers, 'Umar had now become their supreme commander.

2

The Conquest of Iraq and Syria

The direction of the conquests

The direction of the conquests had already been indicated in the time of the Prophet by the marches to Mu'ta and Tabuk, followed by the intended expedition under Usama b. Zayd. Neither the Persians nor the Romans could have long tolerated an independent kingdom in the Arabian Peninsula. In the past, attempts to establish Arab independence had met with defeat and, after defeat, punitive reprisals. The Arabs living in the borderlands and within Syria were Christian and therefore identified with their overlords, the Romans. The Persian imperial court was in some disarray. Following the murder of the Emperor Khosrau II, all his direct male heirs except for the infant Yazdgird were wiped out in fratricidal killings. Therefore, the greater and more imminent danger to the Muslim state was from the direction of the Christian Arab tribes of the Syrian borderlands.

The preparations of the Christian Arabs and their Roman allies were substantial, with the Muslims ill-equipped to match them. Any plans to do so during the caliphate of Abu Bakr had to wait upon the successful conclusion of the so-called 'apostasy wars'. After the death of the Prophet, several tribes in the east and south of the Peninsula (notably, the Banu Hanifa), who had recently sworn allegiance, rejected the authority of the Caliph. This was in effect a relapse by them into *jahiliyya* (barbarism) in both religious and political terms, not so much a move to assert independence as a reversion to subjection once again to Persian overlordship. Their rejection of the Caliph was expressed in the refusal of some to pay the alms tax obligatory upon all Muslims, and in the acceptance by others of evidently false 'prophets' who defined them as tribal communities distinct from the society of Muslims. After a series of brilliant campaigns under Khalid b. al-Walid, rebellion and apostasy were effectively and finally quelled. The Arabs of the Peninsula were united (and would only ever remain so) under the banner of Islam.

At the beginning of 13 AH, as the apostasy wars concluded, Abu Bakr felt able to send a substantial force in the direction of Syria. This force was divided into four separate commands directed at Hims (Emessa), Damascus, Jordan, and Palestine under the leadership, respectively, of Abu 'Ubayda b. al-Jarrah, Yazid b. Abi Sufyan, Shurahbil b. Hasana, and 'Amr b. al-'As. Once they crossed into Roman territory, each of these commanders faced well-organized resistance and counter-attack. To avoid annihilation, they needed to concentrate their forces. They accordingly notified the Caliph in Madina and appealed for urgent reinforcements.

Meanwhile, in the southern Iraq border region, two chieftains of the Wayil clan, as often in the past, exploited the disorder in the Persian court to make northward raids into Persian-held territory. One of them, a very great warrior, Muthanna Shaybani, had become Muslim, although his clansmen were mostly polytheists. He waited upon Abu Bakr in Madina and asked permission to invade Persian territory. Abu Bakr sent him back to his people to first invite them to accept Islam. This they did and then marched into southern Iraq. The Caliph then authorized Khalid b. al-Walid to support them. Under Khalid's command, all the frontier towns under Persian control were quickly taken, including the significant Hira, near the site later designated for the building of Kufa. At this point the plea for reinforcements in Syria reached Abu Bakr, who ordered Khalid to answer it. Khalid left Iraq in the month of Rabi' II, 13 AH, leaving Muthanna in charge.

Khalid's march west from Hira and then northwards into Syria was opposed at many points: it was one of the most dazzling military accomplishments of an outstanding career. The Roman forces, commanded by Theodore, the brother of the Emperor Heraclius, had gathered near Ajnadayn, between Gaza and Jerusalem, and were preparing for a major offensive. Khalid, joining up with Abu 'Ubayda, anticipated and attacked first. The forces of Shurahbil, Yazid, and 'Amr b. al-'As arrived in time to take part in a severely contested battle. Following a victory in which 3,000 Muslims were killed, Khalid marched on to Damascus and besieged the great city.

That was the situation 'Umar inherited when he succeeded Abu Bakr as Caliph: the Romans defending Damascus with resolve while awaiting relief and reinforcements promised by Heraclius; and the Persians gathering themselves to retake the towns they had lost in southern Iraq. To express it briefly: the Arabs who were Muslims in Arabia proper were both united and secure. But elsewhere, the recent gains by Arab/Muslim forces, and the forces themselves, were exposed and vulnerable.

IRAQ

Muthanna was among many chieftains present in Madina to swear allegiance to the new Caliph. He urged that the battle against the fire-worshippers (the Persians) be resumed. The eloquence of 'Umar overcame the doubts of the assembled Arabs, borne of long experience, that they could take and hold Iraq against the Persians, especially without the generalship of Khalid. Then, a senior of the Thaqif tribe, Abu 'Ubayda, in a burst of courage, offered to take on the task. His courage was infectious and many volunteered. 'Umar rewarded the man by appointing him to the command of the 1,000 or so volunteers who left Madina the following day, to be joined by many more on their march. Abu 'Ubayda Thaqafi was not a Companion, that is, he had not accepted Islam in the lifetime of the Prophet. It is a tribute to the authority of Islam, represented in the authority of the Caliph, that Abu 'Ubayda's command was accepted by senior Companions who were a part of the force, as indeed by Muthanna himself, a chieftain of high social standing and proven valour.

The battle of Marwa (the Bridge)

The Persian court had appointed Rustam as Chief Marshal to organize the response to the Arab incursion into Iraq. Rustam's very public preparations had the desired effect of rousing a rebellion against the Arabs, so that they were ousted from all their gains including Hira. He then sent out two advance columns to consolidate control. Abu 'Ubayda, still bursting with zeal, took the initiative and defeated both columns in consecutive pitched battles. Local nobles and landlords promptly reaffirmed their allegiance to the Muslims.

Rustam now sent in his main force of some 4,000, including an elephant corps, under the command of Mardan Shah. This army encamped amid great show of splendour and power at Marwa on the eastern bank of the Euphrates in sight of the Muslims on the opposite bank. Mardan Shah played upon the impetuosity of Abu 'Ubayda, daring the Arabs to cross the river to give battle. Muthanna and other senior officers advised Abu 'Ubayda not to accept this challenge, but obeyed him without question when he insisted. A bridge of boats was built and the Muslims crossed to the opposite bank, where the ground proved unsuitable for any ordered attack or defence. When the Persians' elephants charged, the Muslims' horses were startled and chaos ensued. Abu 'Ubayda dismounted and attacked the elephants on foot. He was killed, as were his brother and seven other Thaqafis, in an exhibition of inspiring courage. But the rout continued. The Muslims' retreat was blocked when the bridge was broken. Many were forced into the river and drowned. Muthanna took command, rallying the Muslims to him. He held access to the bridge until it could be repaired and some remnant of the Muslim army was saved. His valour not only rescued the Muslims from annihilation, it deterred the Persians from following up their victory.

The battle of Buwayb

The battle of the Bridge (dated by one historian to Ramadan, 13 AH) was a catastrophe. Two-thirds of the Muslims were slain or drowned. Many had fled. The consciousness of having done so haunted some to the point where they could not return home for shame. However, 'Umar consoled those fugitives who reached Madina as best he could, and ordered a general mobilization across the whole of Arabia. Muthanna, though grievously wounded, likewise toured the borderlands of southern Iraq urging his clansmen to arms. Over the next months, Christian as well as Muslim tribes gathered in Madina in response to 'Umar's appeal and joined with Muthanna under his command. In Ramadan, 14 AH, the Arabs were encamped on the western bank of the Euphrates at Buwayb. They faced a formidable force including 12,000 horsemen under the command of Mehran b. Mathruya Hamadani.

Mehran crossed the river at dawn to give battle. Muthanna had arranged his forces in several divisions under competent officers and personally toured the lines to enthuse his men. He put himself at the head of the Christian Arabs and aimed a charge at the centre of the advancing Persians, hoping to reach Mehran. Muthanna's brother was slain; so too was one of the Christian chiefs. However, Muthanna would not allow his men to be disheartened. By word and example he rallied the Arabs until they penetrated to the centre of the Persian force. A young warrior of the Taghlab tribe had the honour of slaying Mehran. The demoralized Persians gave up the fight and sought escape. The Arabs barred access to the bridge and the retreating army was annihilated.

The Muslim army soon overran southern Iraq. The more lasting consequence of this battle was that the Arabs lost once and for all their awe of the imperial might of the Sassanids.

The decisive battle: Qadisiya

Stung by their defeat, the Persians set about equipping a massive force to expel the Arabs. Their morale was greatly lifted by the coronation of the sixteen-year-old Yazdgird III as the new emperor. Aware of these developments, 'Umar ordered Muthanna to retreat towards the frontiers of Arabia and concentrate his men there until reinforcements could arrive.

'Umar once more appealed for a general mobilization of the Muslims: the response was overwhelming, with every tribe sending large contingents from as far south as Yemen and Hadramawt. It is apparent—from the scale of 'Umar's preparations, from the seniority in Islam of the men he appointed to divisional command, and from his decision to lead the campaign in person, leaving 'Ali to deputize for him in Madina—that he envisaged a decisive battle for control of southern Iraq. Among the notable men in the army that set out from Madina, no less than 70 were Companions who had taken part in the battle of Badr, 300 who had sworn their allegiance to the Prophet at Hudaybiya, as many again who had accompanied him on the conquest of Makka, and at least 700 were the sons of Companions. There was thus a particular ardour and concentration for the cause of Islam, a feeling that this was not a campaign intended to exploit a military opportunity or to rescue a venture that had not quite succeeded, but instead a test of themselves as Muslims to see if they could project and impress the rule of Islam.

The issue of a war, whatever the quality of belief in its aims, cannot be known before it is fought. Several of the most senior Companions counselled the Caliph against taking the field in person. No man so fully represented the rule of Islam as 'Umar and if he fell in battle, so the Companions reasoned, the consequences for the Muslims as a united power would be grave. 'Umar agreed to this counsel. As Abu 'Ubayda and Khalid were preoccupied in Syria, and 'Ali refused the general command, 'Umar accepted the suggestion of 'Abd al-Rahman b. 'Awf to appoint Sa'd b. Abi Waqqas, a Badr veteran held in universal esteem. 'Umar, uneasy about Sa'd's experience as a military tactician, insisted on organizing the expedition himself, specifying beforehand the divisions of the army into combat and support units, even each of the halts between Madina and Iraq. Further, the Caliph required Sa'd to submit, as far as practicable, regular, detailed reports of the disposition of his own and enemy forces, and to seek his authorization before undertaking any major operation.

On the march towards Hira, Sa'd was joined by the forces of Muthanna, now under the command of his brother, Mu'ama: the great Muthanna had succumbed to his battle-wounds but, through Mu'ama, bequeathed much valuable information and counsel to Sa'd. The Muslims, numbering in all around 30,000, fixed camp, on the direct orders of 'Umar, at Qadisiya, a small township about twenty miles from the site of Kufa. 'Umar knew this place from his travels to be supplied with canals and bridges that made it well-suited for defence. To refresh his memory he commanded that a detailed map should be sent to him. On the way to Qadisiya, Sa'd was able to capture unopposed a large military arsenal abandoned by the Persians. His scouts reported that the Persian army, some 60,000 men, including large cavalry battalions and an elephant corps, under the command of Rustam, had now gathered at Sabat. Sa'd informed 'Umar, who ordered that an embassy be sent to Mada'in, the Persians' capital, to invite them to accept the rule of Islam. At the same time, he sent word to Abu 'Ubayda on the Syrian front to dispatch what reinforcements he could to support Sa'd.

Sa'd chose fourteen men for their dignity of bearing and soundness of judgement and speech, and sent them to Yazdgird under the command of Nu'man b. Maqran. The Persians of the court received the Muslim envoys with all the procedures, ceremonies and attitudes of people long used to the exercise of power over inferiors, confident of the antiquity and depth of their wealth and cultural tradition. They inevitably regarded the Arabs as uncouth barbarians who had, for the sake of a rash military adventure, sacrificed all sense of their place in the scheme of things. They doubted neither the Arabs' courage nor their capacity to inflict heavy casualties. Equally, they did not doubt that the Arabs would be crushed. In sum, the Persians must have expected from the Muslims' embassy some mixture of vaunting threats and demands for money or territory or both. What they cannot have expected is that Arabs would presume to come to them with a teaching, ideas, a civilizing mission. Nu'man dwelt briefly upon the stirring clarity of the Islamic creed, the affirmation and completion of the Divine revelation to man through the Prophets, then urged the young Emperor to accept Islam or choose between *jizya* or the arbitration of battle. It is not difficult to imagine the outrage of Yazdgird, whom his court addressed as 'the King of kings', at the Muslims' presumption. He reminded the Arabs of their backwardness and poverty, their constant feuding with one another, their inferiority in arms, the long history of their subjugation to Persian dominion. Mughira b. Zurara answered for the Muslims. He confirmed the faults and weaknesses of his people only as a thing of the past. Now, all had changed:

It is true that we were wretched and erring; that we slew one another; that we buried infant daughters alive. But God sent to us a Prophet who was the noblest among us from the noblest lineage. At first we opposed him. He spoke the truth and we belied him; he advanced and we receded. However, little by little, he touched a chord in our hearts. Whatever he said, he said at the bidding of God; and whatever he did, likewise. He commanded us to offer this religion to the whole world. Those who embraced Islam came into the same rights as we enjoyed, those who refused but agreed to pay *jizya* came under the protection of Islam. Those who accepted neither had to face battle. (Ibn al-Athir, *Kamil*, 2:457)

Yazdgird dismissed the Muslim ambassadors with contempt. His commander-in-chief was less clear-cut. For the next three months Rustam failed to move his troops towards the Muslim position and twice called for negotiations. On both occasions the Muslim ambassadors defied him, refusing either to be frightened or bought off. Sa'd acted with the utmost prudence. Instead of offering pitched battle, he attacked and occupied outlying settlements, forcing local landowners to appeal to the Emperor to protect them. Others defected to the Muslim side; there were desertions too from the Persian troops. Since delay was having a bad effect on the morale of his forces, Rustam had, in the end, no choice but to attack the Muslims' well-defended position. Once he had accepted this, he moved with commendable decisiveness. He marched to Qadisiya, had the intervening channel of water choked up and converted into a road in a single night, and by noon directly confronted the Muslim battle lines. If the display of energy had been intended to revive the spirits of his troops, it surely succeeded: it is recorded that several thousands of the infantry chained themselves together to show solidarity and commitment.

Sa'd was afflicted with sciatica and so did not take part directly in the ensuing battle. However, he closely observed and guided the action from a vantage-point in the rear of the field. The Persians opened the general fighting with a charge from their elephant corps, each elephant carrying a howdah filled with archers and lancers. The charging elephants caused the Arabs' horses in the front line to shy and panic. When the ranks of infantry behind them also began to stagger and press back, Sa'd mobilized archers and small squadrons of cavalry against the elephants. Thus, the Muslims' lines were broken and re-formed several times during the battle, with the Persians unable to take and hold any ground. The contending forces withdrew at dusk.

Some 6,000 reinforcements from the Syrian front under the command of Sa'd's brother, Hashim b. 'Utba, were now approach-ing Qadisiya. The main bulk of this force were led in, before the recommencement of fighting on the second day, by Qa'qa'. He deliberately had them appear on the battlefield in waves so that their number would seem to the Persians unending. Further, he had some camels wrapped in billowing cloths stretched over wooden frames, and these artificial mammoths served for a time, like the Persians' elephants, to panic the horses in the enemy lines. As on the first day, the battle surged to and fro, the Muslims inflicting heavier casualties on their opponents than they suffered themselves, but without by any means achieving a breakthrough. Under cover of night, Qa'qa' sent squadrons of cavalry and infantry back in the direction of Syria, with instructions to reappear on the battlefield, again in waves, to create an impression of mul-titudes of reinforcements.

During the third day's battle, Hashim b. 'Utba entered the

field with 700 fresh horsemen, further heartening the Muslim forces with news of the conquest of Damascus. The Muslims learnt to overcome the Persians' elephants by aiming lances and arrows at their eyes and little by little began to advance. The energy and ferocity of their attack intensified through dusk into the night. Finally, Qa'qa', gathering a band of the most renowned warriors from several clans, made a drive towards Rustam, the commander-in-chief of the Persian army. Others soon joined this rush and Rustam, along with the body of men protecting his position, was forced to retreat. He was caught and slain while trying to swim across a brook. As news of this calamity for the Persians spread, it demoralized them as much as it heartened the Muslims. The battle of Qadisiya concluded in a rout. Many of the Persian officers refused to leave the field and fought on until they were killed. Others fled and tried to reorganize elsewhere the ragged remnants of the once-mighty Persian army.

The capture of Mada'in and Hulwan

Sa'd understood the need to press home the victory. He therefore ordered a march on Babal where, according to his scouts, the main bulk of the retreating Persian army had regrouped. He moved warily, sending columns ahead of his march to clear the way for the main concentration of the Muslims' forces. The forward columns were opposed at Burs, but with little conviction. Burs was surrendered on terms of the *jizya*, with the local landowners assisting the conquerors in building bridges across the waterways that defended Babal. From Babal (taken in 15 AH), the Persians retreated to Kutha, the place where Nimrod was thought to have imprisoned the Prophet Abraham. Sa'd visited the dungeon, at that time preserved as a shrine, and prayed for peace upon Abraham, and reflected upon the mutability of all human affairs. The Muslims moved on from Kutha to take Bahra-Sher after a two-month siege, leaving only the Tigris barring their way to the cities of Yazdgird's capital, Mada'in.

The Persians had destroyed all boats and bridges as they crossed.

Sa'd himself led the famous charge into the waters of the Tigris which so stupefied the enemy that most of them abandoned all hopes of resistance and fled. Only the Persians' commander, accompanied by a few resolute officers and a small band of archers, struggled briefly and in vain to halt the Muslims' advance. Yazdgird, his family, and all his court had already fled and removed to Hulwan when Sa'd entered the capital. The empty streets and deserted palaces moved him profoundly and he called to mind verses of the Qur'an whose meaning is: 'They left many a garden, fountain, park, arbour and riches they used to enjoy. Thus do We put in possession thereof a later generation' (44.25–8). All the priceless treasures and heirlooms of the Sassanid 'Kings of kings' were gathered up and sent back to Madina along with one-fifth of the rest of the spoils, the remaining four-fifths being divided up among the troops. The first service of Friday prayers in Iraq was held in the palace of Khosrau I, his throne serving as a temporary pulpit. It is a matter of historical record that Sa'd, an eminent Companion who had enjoyed the company of the Prophet over very many years, permitted the statuary in the palace to remain in place.

Persian resistance was no longer coordinated by or in the name of Yazdgird. However, loyal Persian nobles, officers, and landowners, under the command of Kharzad, the brother of Rustam, assembled a large army at the city of Jalula. Expecting to be attacked, Kharzad made the most careful preparations, surrounding the city with a moat and covering the accesses to the city with dense thornwood and spikes to impede horses. Under specific instruction from 'Umar, Sa'd sent a force of 12,000 divided into units, one to be led by Qa'qa', under the general command of Hashim b. 'Utba; other senior officers were also named by 'Umar. The ensuing siege lasted several months into the year 16 AH, with the Persians from time to time making impressively courageous sallies against the besiegers. On the occasion of one of these, a sudden heavy dust storm forced the Persians to retreat and, in the storm, great numbers of them fell into their own defensive moat. In order to complete the retreat successfully, they had to fill in the moat at certain points. Qa'qa' seized the chance to launch a fierce attack

that took his contingent into the entrance of the city but separated
them from the main body of the Muslims. Qa'qa' had it proclaimed
that the Muslims' commander-in-chief had entered the city. The
Persians, no doubt over-mindful of their many recent defeats,
began to panic. However, their escape was prevented by the very
thornwood they had thrown in the way of the advancing Muslims
and many were captured or slain.

Sa'd moved up to Jalula, sending Qa'qa' on to take Hulwan.
Perhaps to ensure the escape of Yazdgird and his family to Rayy,
a few squadrons of Persians engaged the Muslims a few miles
from the city. When these were defeated, Qa'qa' entered Hulwan
and had peace proclaimed by beat of drum. Many nobles and
landowners from the surrounding areas came to hear and accept
the terms of the *jizya*. The conquest of Iraq was secure.

SYRIA

The capture of Damascus

Abu 'Ubayda was commander-in-chief on the Syrian front. However,
the counsel of Khalid b. al-Walid undoubtedly prevailed in any
question of tactics or strategy. Certainly it was Khalid who organized
the siege of Damascus. All the forces of the Muslims in Syria
were focused on taking this city, long admired by the Arabs for
its grandeur and magnificence and known personally to many of
them because their trade caravans frequented it. Khalid surrounded
the Syrian capital on all sides, assigning one each of the four
sectors to Shurahbil, 'Amr b. al-'As, and Abu 'Ubayda, with himself
covering the eastern gate. The citizens were hoping that a great
Roman army from Hims (Emessa), promised by Heraclius, would
relieve them, and that, in the meantime, the Syrian winter would
soon chill the Muslims' commitment to maintaining a rigorous
siege. They were disappointed in both expectations. As there were
many Christian Arabs in Damascus, it was not difficult to send
spies into the Muslim encampments: but these could report no
relaxation in the Muslims' discipline or resolve. As for the relief

force from Hims, Khalid too was expecting it and had positioned troops one march from Damascus to intercept and divert it.

On the birth of a son to the city governor, citizens and soldiers indulged themselves in drunken celebrations. According to one account, Muslim troops under Khalid's command, and following his personal example, swam the moat on inflated skins, scaled the walls with rope ladders, quickly overpowered the guards, and opened the gates. According to another account, Khalid was informed of the drunken stupor of the guards, and the ladders were supplied, by a Christian from within the city. As soon as the Muslims had gained access, the citizens raised the alarm and, deciding all was lost, opened the other gates also. The surrender was accepted by Abu 'Ubayda even while Khalid and his troops were fighting in the eastern quarter. It is a considerable tribute to the magnanimity of Khalid, and his sense of duty, that he honoured the terms of peaceful surrender for the whole city, forbidding the taking of spoils or prisoners. Damascus was captured in the month of Rajab, 14 AH, the siege having lasted in all six months.

The battle of Fihl (Pella)

Following this victory, the Muslims turned south to secure the province of Jordan. At Baysan, about eighteen miles from the province's chief city, Tibriya (Tiberias), a large Roman army had assembled, reinforced by the troops diverted from the relief of Damascus, with further reinforcements expected. The Muslim forces encamped at Fihl (Pella) on the western side of the Lake of Tiberias (Sea of Galilee), with dams and channels drawn from the lake separating them from the Romans. The latter, not wishing to engage in battle until all the forces they expected had arrived, broke the dams so that a continuous stretch of water and mud separated them from the Muslim camp. As the Muslims showed no sign of being deterred, the Romans offered negotiations. Abu 'Ubayda appointed Mu'adh b. Jabal as his ambassador. The Christians sought in vain to impress Mu'adh with a grand, ceremonial reception, with the long history of Roman conquests, the prestige and absolute power of their Emperor, and the limitless military resources at his disposal. Also in vain, they urged the Arabs, through Mu'adh, to turn their lust for conquest upon the Persians. Mu'adh simply invited the Romans to accept Islam and become the Muslims' brothers instead of their enemies, or to accept their protection under the terms of the *jizya*, failing which the issue would be determined by battle. He concluded:

You take pride in acknowledging yourselves subjects of an emperor who can dispose of your lives or property at will. But the one whom we have made our ruler does not enjoy such precedence over us. If he committed fornication, he would be flogged; if he committed theft, his hands would be cut off . . . . He does not think himself greater than we are, not does he prefer himself in the booty God has given us. (al-Azdi, 119)

Mu'adh flatly rejected the Romans' offer to cede the district of Balqa (a part of Jordan contiguous with Arabia) to the Arabs if they would transfer their ambitions to Persia. The Romans then sent an embassy directly to Abu 'Ubayda, but this too failed. An account of these negotiations was relayed to the Caliph in Madina, who urged them to remain steadfast in the cause of Islam.

Instead of taking advantage of their superior numbers and launching a full offensive, the Romans sent out separate units of cavalry and infantry in consecutive assaults against the Muslims. Khalid quickly grasped the tentative quality of these tactics and urged Abu 'Ubayda to prepare for a wholehearted attack on the Romans' positions the following day. Khalid took command of the vanguard, with Hashim b. 'Utba and Mu'adh b. Jabal commanding the left and right flanks of the Muslim troops. The Romans attacked again in the same manner as on the previous day, but this time Khalid allowed his division to be driven back. The Romans, elated with this success, pushed more men into the attack against Khalid, who continued to retreat slowly until the advancing Romans were separated in sufficient numbers from their main forces. He then manoeuvred around them, turned, and attacked. The Muslim

commanders on the flanks simultaneously charged the Romans'
now exposed centre. The archers positioned to prevent such a charge
might have halted the Muslims but for the sheer determination
and ferocity of, in particular, Hashim b. 'Utba and his force. The
Romans scattered in disorder, suffering heavy losses.

The rest of the province of Jordan was quickly taken with
either token resistance or none at all. Abu 'Ubayda received instructions from 'Umar about the terms of peace, especially in regard
to the treatment of the conquered peoples and the disposal of
land.

The capture of Hims (Emessa)

Of Syria proper, the only important cities that remained to be
captured were Antioch, Heraclius' present capital, Jerusalem, and
Hims (Emessa). As Antioch and Jerusalem were better defended,
the Muslim commanders chose to attack Hims first. On the way,
Khalid took the fortress of Ba'albak before facing and defeating
the Roman garrison from Hims at Josiah. As a precaution, he
sent columns into the areas around Hims to seek out any remnants
of the scattered Roman forces, before laying siege to the city. The
citizens, as in Damascus, expected the harsh winter cold to weaken
the Muslims' resolve and their own Emperor to mount a rescue.
(It seems Heraclius did try to mobilize troops from Upper
Mesopotamia (Jazira) but these were blocked by a detachment
from the Muslim armies fighting the Persians.) After some weeks,
Hims capitulated. Following its capture, Abu 'Ubayda and Khalid
took, in quick succession, Hama, Shizar, Ladhqiya, and Qinisirin.
They met significant resistance only at the ancient Phoenician
city of Ladhqiya (Amathna).

Abu 'Ubayda would have proceeded directly to attempt Antioch
but was commanded not to do so by the Caliph. He therefore
sent his senior commanders to garrison the towns and cities that
had been taken against potential rebellion. Khalid was stationed
in Damascus, 'Amr b. al-'As in Jordan, while Abu 'Ubayda remained
at Hims.

The decisive battle: Yarmuk

Heraclius, perhaps feeling that his armies in Syria had not fought convincingly, was inclined to let the province go. When he asked why, despite superiority in numbers and equipment, his forces had been defeated, his counsellors spoke of the superior morale of the Muslims, their discipline of prayer and fasting, their zeal for their religion and resolve to see its rule established. No argument could have been better calculated to persuade the Emperor to retake Syria: it was barely a decade since he had driven out the Persians and recovered the Holy Land for Christian rule. He rose to the challenge of recovering it a second time, issuing a command to every province of his empire to send all available troops and equipment to Antioch. The force thus assembled comprised many nationalities, including some Arabs who had yet to go over to the side of the Muslims, but its overall character was that of a Christian army which, when it took the field, marched with the symbols of their faith held aloft.

Just as, during the Persians' preparations for a counter-offensive, the territories in southern Iraq rebelled against Muslim control, so too the areas of Jordan and Palestine, anticipating the imminent return of the Romans, rebelled against the Muslims. Remarkably, the populous cities did not welcome the prospect of a return to Roman rule. Among the Muslim generals, opinion was initially divided about how to respond. Eventually, the consistently reliable strategic wisdom of Khalid prevailed to achieve a consensus: the Muslims were to leave first Hims, then Damascus, and retreat to the river Yarmuk, where they could concentrate their forces in defensible terrain close to Arabia. At the Yarmuk, they could hope that reinforcements might reach them in time to avert the worst or, if the worst came, they could retreat in orderly formation. 'Umar was grieved that his generals, not before intimidated by heavy odds, had chosen to withdraw. It was a consolation to all Muslims in Madina that the decision to do so had been reached by consensus; and a cause of renewed conviction in the virtue of Islamic rule that the non-Muslim citizens of both the great cities of Hims and Damascus had promised to bar their gates to the Roman troops. 'Umar could muster and dispatch a contingent of only one thousand to reinforce the Muslims at Yarmuk. He rejected the advice of some of the Companions that they should all go, with the Caliph at their head, to die if need be with their brother Muslims.

The Yarmuk (Hieromax) is a tributary of the river Jordan flowing on the east side of the Sea of Galilee, with other tributaries nearby forming many steep valleys and ravines. Khalid positioned the Muslim forces, numbering in all between 30,000 and 35,000, with their left flank protected by the ravines and a clear field behind them in case a retreating manoeuvre became necessary. The Romans, under the command of Bahan, outnumbered the Muslims three to one. As news of these odds reached Madina, there was understandable concern, but further withdrawal was not a wise option. There was, to begin with, no assurance that the Romans would not invade Arabia itself. More important, the progress of Islam among the Arab tribes of Syria, not to speak of the Arabs of Iraq, might have been halted or reversed. In sum, the Muslims had to win at Yarmuk. With a letter sent to Abu 'Ubayda, 'Umar had the messenger convey these words (al-Azdi, 184): 'O Muslims! You must meet the enemy in the right spirit: attack them in the manner of lions while regarding them as feebler than ants. Then we certainly believe you will overcome them.' 'Umar's letter arrived at the same time as the reinforcements dispatched earlier, greatly boosting the Muslims' morale.

The Romans' immediate purpose was to force the Arabs out of Syria altogether: if they would leave without a difficult battle so much the better. Bahan therefore offered negotiations. Abu 'Ubayda deputed Khalid to represent the Muslims.

Bahan spoke first in praise of the doctrines of the Christian religion. After that, he argued that the Romans had given no cause for the Arabs to be attacking Syria. Rather, since they had for so many years treated the Arabs resident in Syria and the adjacent borderlands with generosity, the Arabs as a whole should be disposed to favour, not oppose, the Romans. Even so, the Roman Emperor was minded to be magnanimous, to overlook the Arabs' barbarous ingratitude, and had authorized a payment to the Arabs' commanders and to each of their men if they would withdraw to their own lands.

Of course, such terms were unthinkable for the Muslims. In reply, Khalid pointed out that if the Romans had treated the Arabs well it was only to proselytize them while extending the dominion of the Roman Emperor. He explained that the barbarism of which the Romans accused the Arabs was a thing of the past. They had entered Syria as Muslims to establish there the rule of Islam. Khalid then expounded the strict monotheism that the Prophet had taught to the Muslims, and the principles of equity and justice that faith in Islam entailed. He concluded with the offer to treat the Romans as brothers if they accepted Islam or to protect them if they accepted the *jizya*. As the Romans refused, Khalid returned to the Muslim encampment and prepared for the inevitable battle the next day.

He divided the troops at his disposal into thirty-six more or less equal units of a thousand men and spread them, using the terrain to maximum advantage, in such a way that each unit could move out to support another as the need arose. The centre of the Muslim lines was under the general command of Abu 'Ubayda, the left under Yazid b. Abi Sufyan, the right under 'Amr b. al-'As and Shurahbil. Khalid put himself in command of the remaining units, held towards the rear, whose speed and mobility was to prove decisive. The encampments of the women were, as usual, behind the battle lines. But, of this battle, the sources record that many women fought in the ranks, with notably heroic deeds attributed to the mother and sister of Mu'awiya b. Abi Sufyan.

The sources also record that verses of the Qur'an were recited over and over by the warriors before and during the battle, particularly those that affirm the virtue and reward hereafter of true believers who offer their lives for Islam. No doubt, this was in part prompted by the fact that priests and bishops accompanied the Romans' assault, holding aloft their crosses and invoking the aid of Jesus Christ. But the Muslims were surely well aware of the odds they faced and all that was at stake for them.

At Ajnadayn, the Romans had been tentative in their attacks;

not so at Yarmuk. They moved with assurance, speed, and in great numbers, preceded by archers. Under continual pressure, the right flank of the Muslim lines was split and pushed back as far as the women's encampments. There, the women (who came out brandishing tent-poles) forced the units in retreat to turn and stand. Led by Mu'adh b. Jabal, they held long enough for another unit, commanded by Hajjaj, the chieftain of the Zubayd clan, to come to their aid. The sheer courage and resolve of the Muslims' resistance began to tell on the Romans, whose forward thrust came to a standstill. The remaining units on the Muslim right flank also held steady, their valour and the terrain combining to neutralize the Romans' advantage in numbers. Khalid decided this was his moment to strike. He led out his unit in a charge of such suddenness and speed that it cut through the advancing Romans and into the centre of their positions, where the Romans' general commanders were stationed. Many eminent and well-known Muslims were slain in this magnificent charge: particularly remembered is 'Ikrima, the son of Abu Jahl, the most fanatical of those Quraysh nobles who had hated and sought to kill the Prophet of Islam.

The day might have been decided by this one brilliant and heroic manoeuvre had the Romans not launched a vigorous assault on the Muslims' left flank. The officers and commanders stood firm, in particular, Yazid and Mu'awiya, the sons of Abu Sufyan, who was present on the battlefield urging them not to disgrace Islam. However, the troops they commanded—mostly clansmen of Lakhm and Ghassan, former subjects of the Romans still in awe of their military reputation—fell apart in disorder. They were pushed back towards the tents of the women who, coming out to fight alongside the men, hectored them for their cowardice. Other units from the centre and right (under Sa'id b. Zayd, 'Amr b. al-'As and Shurahbil) rushed to support the left flank and the Romans were slowed down and even pushed back. Then, in a manoeuvre similar to Khalid's, Qays b. Habira led a fierce cavalry charge from the rear of the left flank, which broke the Romans' formations. As they fell back, the Muslims regrouped and moved forward. A final charge, led out from the centre of the Muslim

lines by Sa'id b. Zayd, reduced the Romans to panicked flight.
Huge numbers perished in the ravines and steep valleys as well
as on the field. Of the Muslims, 3,000 gave their lives for the
victory at Yarmuk.

No battle fought in this region before or since has had such
lasting consequences as Yarmuk: the history of the southern
Mediterranean was permanently changed by it. When news reached
'Umar in Madina, he prostrated before God in gratitude for putting
an end to his sleepless anxiety. He was not alone in grasping the
full significance of this battle. Heraclius was in Antioch when he
received the news of the disaster his army had suffered. He bade
farewell to the beautiful, fertile province of Syria and removed
his capital to Constantinople. In abandoning Syria, he must have
known that he was effectively abandoning the Roman territories
in Upper Mesopotamia (Jazira) as well.

The capture of Jerusalem

The Muslims were welcomed back into Damascus and Hims, from
where they proceeded quickly to take the whole of Syria. As
resistance was minimal, there was very little or no bloodshed, most
cities surrendering on the terms of the *jizya* after a few days. Khalid
re-took Qinisirin, 'Iyad b. Ghanam captured Aleppo, clearing the
way for Abu 'Ubayda to take Antioch. At Bughras, on the frontier
of Asia Minor, a number of Arab clans who had served as auxiliaries
with the Romans put up stiff resistance before accepting defeat.
Once the northern end of the province was secure, Abu 'Ubayda
marched southwards to Jerusalem, the one major city in Syria which
had refused to surrender. It had been besieged by 'Amr b. al-'As
since Yarmuk. The collapse of Aleppo and Antioch in particular,
and now the approach of Abu 'Ubayda, finally convinced the citizens
of Jerusalem that further resistance was useless. They agreed
to hand over the city only if the Caliph in person accepted the
surrender and ratified the terms of peace associated with it.

After taking counsel with senior Companions, 'Umar made
the decision to go to Syria. Accompanied by a few Ansar and

Muhajirun, he left in the month of Rajab, 16 AH, appointing 'Ali
to take charge in his absence. All the senior generals who had
taken part in the Syrian campaign gathered to receive the Caliph
at Jabiya. Whereas 'Umar was dressed in the plain, coarse cloth
he had always used since his conversion to Islam, he remarked
with anger the fine robes that adorned the figures of his generals,
in particular Yazid b. Abi Sufyan and Khalid. It is recorded that
he sprang from his mount and pelted them with stones. He was
somewhat appeased to learn that, beneath this finery, the great
warriors were still wearing their cuirasses. However, they failed
to persuade him to make a grand entrance into Jerusalem. They
were anxious not to expose the Caliph to the contemptuous glances
of the citizens. Jerusalem was (with the possible exception of the
coastal fortress of Qaysaria (Caesarea), not taken till 19 AH) the
most Hellenized of all the major population centres in Syria—
the associated attitudes of cultural superiority in part explain
the city's stubborn resistance to conquest by Arabs as well as the
Arabs' desire not to appear unimpressive. For his part, 'Umar
received the deputation from Jerusalem, formally confirmed the
terms of peaceful surrender, and entered the city, all in his habitual
dress. In the same over-patched robe he made his way to the
arch of David. There he recited verses from the Qur'an which
describe how that Messenger of God and just, victorious king of
his people, bowed to God as His humble servant. He then visited
the great churches of the Christians and other sites in the city,
the most important being those sites where the Mosques of Aqsa
and 'Umar now stand.

The adhan in Jerusalem

During his stay in Jerusalem, the Caliph received a complaint
from Bilal, Companion of the Prophet and his mu'adhdhin, that
while officers ate white bread and fowl, their men could not get
even simple fare. The officers, when challenged, said that such
food was as cheap here as brown bread and dates in the Hijaz.
'Umar could urge but not compel them to be more frugal. However,

he issued a decree requiring that the ordinary soldiers should henceforth be supplied with free rations in addition to their regular pay and share in spoils of war.

Perhaps this decree so pleased Bilal that he could not refuse the request 'Umar put to him to make the call to prayer. After the death of the Prophet, Bilal had always said that he would not call the *adhan* for any other. When his beautiful, familiar voice rang out over Jerusalem, it carried the minds and hearts of the Companions back to the time when the Prophet was amongst them. They reflected on what they had lost and could never again recover, no matter how great their courage or perseverance—his blessed company and the Revelation that came to him in response to their questions, teaching and consoling them and raising altogether the horizons of their world. How small were the gains in Syria when balanced against that loss! Many of the Companions were reduced to weeping. Their leader, the disciplinarian 'Umar, who had so recently pelted his own generals with stones in a burst of indignation at their expensive clothes, was seized by a fit of sobbing which for a long while he could not overcome.

The year of plague and famine

Towards the end of 17 AH a virulent plague broke out and spread from Amwas in Syria through that province and touched Egypt and parts of Iraq. On hearing of it, 'Umar travelled to the area to see what might be done to suppress it. At Surgh, Abu 'Ubayda and other senior Muslims met the Caliph to give counsel. It was widely agreed that it was imprudent for the Caliph himself to remain where he might become infected. When 'Umar made the decision to return to Madina, Abu 'Ubayda allowed himself to ask: "'Umar, do you run away from God's Will?' The Caliph answered calmly: 'Yes, I fly from God's Will but towards God's Will' (Ibn al-Athir, *Kamil*, 2:559–60).

From Madina, 'Umar sent a letter recalling Abu 'Ubayda to the capital but he refused to come. In a second letter, 'Umar ordered Abu 'Ubayda to move his men to Jabiya where the climate was less damp. Abu 'Ubayda complied with this order but had already caught the infection. Knowing that his death was imminent, he appointed Mu'adh b. Jabal to succeed him. 'Amr b. al-'As counselled Mu'adh to disperse the troops in high ground where the purer air might save them from the plague. Mu'adh refused. He argued in a sermon that the plague should be understood as a mercy from God. He did not lose this belief either when his own son caught the plague and died, nor when he himself succumbed. He died in a rapture of certainty that this earthly life is no more than a veil before the Divine vision.

Before he died, Mu'adh nominated as his successor 'Amr b. al-'As, who immediately ordered the troops to disperse in the mountains. Thereafter, the plague subsided: Muslims had died in great numbers, leaving many widows and orphans, and much property unclaimed and uncared for.

Leaving 'Ali in charge in Madina, 'Umar travelled to Syria to supervise the welfare and administrative rearrangements inevitable after the deaths of so many Muslims, who included leading figures, Abu 'Ubayda, Mu'adh and Yazid b. Abi Sufyan the best known among them. He broke his journey in a monastery at Ella where he asked a monk to mend his threadbare shirt. This the kindly monk did and, as discreetly as he could, presented the Caliph with a new shirt. But 'Umar refused the gift, saying that his old shirt served him well as an absorbent of perspiration. Then, accompanied by several of the Companions, 'Umar spent some days in each of the province's major centres, putting affairs in order. He established military stations at the frontiers, made appointments to the posts that had fallen vacant, arranged for the troops to receive the pay due to them, and put the heirs of those who had died in possession of their lawful inheritance. Significantly, 'Umar appointed Mu'awiya b. Abi Sufyan as governor of Syria.

Arabia was visited in the same year (18 AH) by severe drought and famine. The indefatigable energy of 'Umar, who organized caravans of relief supplies from Iraq and Syria and personally supervised their distribution throughout the Peninsula, saved countless lives. The plague in Syria and the famine in Arabia were undoubtedly calamities for the Muslims. They may have helped to accelerate 'Umar's major administrative reform of the period, namely the general census of Muslims, and the *Diwan* or register of servants of the state, on the basis of which salaries and allowances were calculated and disbursed.

The deposition of Khalid

Few Muslims would have disputed that the conquest of Syria, if it could properly be credited to a man, deserved to be credited to the one whom the Prophet himself had honoured with the title of 'Sword of God'. The presence of Khalid on a battlefield was a factor in the morale of the Muslim forces. Further, others learnt military skills and tactics from association with him: by the end of the Syrian campaigns he was the very best of an excellent group of commanders. Why should such a popular and successful general be deposed?

'Umar cannot have desired it, but he had it done. Khalid's success meant that he acquired large administrative duties in addition to the duties of a commander in battle. In the year 17 AH, 'Umar called for detailed reports from Khalid on all expenditures from state funds entrusted to him. Khalid refused to supply these reports on the ground that such reports had not been required during the caliphate of Abu Bakr. Of course circumstances had changed since then: a state treasury had been set up and the proper administration of its large funds necessitated formal accounting procedures. 'Umar insisted and, when Khalid refused to comply, reduced him to a junior command under Abu 'Ubayda.

Later in the same year, it was brought to 'Umar's attention that Khalid had made a present or payment of 10,000 dirhams to a poet. In notifying Abu 'Ubayda, Khalid's immediate superior, 'Umar pointed out that, if the expenditure had been made from public funds, Khalid was guilty of breach of trust, if from his private wealth, he was guilty of extravagance. 'Umar sent a messenger from Madina to challenge Khalid in public about the improper expenditure: if he admitted the charge, the matter was to be taken no further. 'Umar could rely upon Khalid, if he recognized the offence, both to put it right and never to repeat it. But Khalid chose to maintain a dignified silence. The Caliph's messenger then removed Khalid's turban and bound it around his neck, thus symbolizing his deposition from command. It is recorded that not a murmur of complaint issued from the great general's lips. Perhaps, in the moment, his feeling of hurt overpowered him. In Hims, however, he allowed himself to observe in a public speech that the Caliph had recognized him as a chief in Syria but then, once he had conquered the whole of the province, dismissed him. An ordinary soldier got up to remark: 'Be careful of what you say, Commander! Such words might breed sedition.' Khalid, to his great credit, replied: 'Indeed so, except that sedition cannot grow while 'Umar lives!' (Abu Yusuf, 148).

In Madina, Khalid called upon 'Umar in order to express his feelings to him. He said: 'By God, 'Umar, you are unkind to me.' Khalid agreed to have his wealth from spoils of war assessed and to refund to the state treasury any surplus over 60,000 dirhams. As a surplus was found, Khalid duly handed it over. 'Umar said to him: 'By God, Khalid, you are indeed dear to me and I hold you in honourable esteem' (Tabari, 4:68; see trans., 13:108). After that, 'Umar notified all provincial governors to have it proclaimed that Khalid had not been dismissed because of any breach of trust or because the Caliph had any cause of offence against him, but because the people had grown to depend too much upon Khalid when they should depend, instead, upon God who disposed all events, both victory and defeat.

This incident illustrates the strength of character of both men and the greatness of Islam in shaping their characters and reconciling them within a purpose nobler than themselves. We may note, before returning to the narrative of the military campaigns, that Khalid's aunt (the daughter of his grandfather, Hisham b. al-Mughira) was 'Umar's mother. How far 'Umar, in particular, had travelled from the times before Islam, when the demands of such a relationship might have outweighed a moral duty!

3

The Extension of the Conquests

Campaigning did not stop after the capture of Jerusalem. Nevertheless, the pace of military events did slow down on the northern front in Syria and, after the capture of Hulwan, also on the front against the Persians. In spite of the upheavals brought on by plague and famine, and in spite of the dismissal of Khalid, the Muslims did not lose any significant territory after the battles of Yarmuk and Qadisiya. On the contrary, they were able greatly to extend their conquests.

The conquest of Jazira

Jazira is the later Arabic name for Upper Mesopotamia, the broad stretch of territory between the Tigris and Euphrates, most of it now the northern part of modern Iraq. The area had been contested many times by the Romans and Persians. In the campaign ending in 6 AH, Heraclius had driven the Persians back to the southern and eastern ends of the territory but the border between the two empires remained uncertain. When the Muslim forces entered Jazira it was from both directions, from southern Iraq and Syria. Some historians indeed regard the earliest incursions into Jazira as part of the battle for Iraq.

After Qadisiya, there was no immediate threat of any centrally organized effort by the Persians to regain Iraq. However, individual

Persian nobles continued to hope for means to throw out the Arabs. After the fall of Mada'in, the first Persian province to rise up against the Muslims was Persian Jazira. Notified of this by Sa'd b. Abi Waqqas, 'Umar ordered an expedition to counter the threat, nominating 'Abdullah b. al-Mu'tam as its commander. 'Abdullah marched north as far as the city of Takrit, besieging it for some months in the year 16 AH. He failed in twenty-four attempts to storm the city. 'Abdullah then sent secret missions to the Arab clans fighting with their Persian overlords, to persuade them over to the Muslim side. Victory for the Muslims came quickly after 'Abdullah's emissaries succeeded in this task. The Persian forces were drawn out of the city to attack the Muslims. As they did so, they found themselves being charged from behind by their former Arab auxiliaries, and were then completely routed.

Some time after 'Umar's return to Madina from Jerusalem, he received word from Abu 'Ubayda that a strong force was marching on Hims from the Roman part of Jazira. The Caliph had, in anticipation of such an eventuality, created reserve forces that could be mobilized quickly. He ordered a contingent of cavalry stationed at Kufa to hasten directly to the defence of Hims; another to impede the march of the Jaziri forces; and a third to attack Nisibin. At the same time he sent a deputation to urge the Arab clans settled in Jazira to repudiate their allegiance to the Romans. 'Umar then underlined the urgency of the situation by himself setting out for Damascus.

In the event, Hims was not besieged in any strict sense of the word. The support the Jaziris had expected from Constantinople did not materialize. Abu 'Ubayda had posted troops in sufficient numbers outside the city to deter a siege. When the Jaziris learnt that their own territory was in danger of imminent attack by the Muslims from Iraq, they abandoned the idea of besieging Hims. Meanwhile, the Arabs serving with the Christian Jaziris had sent word in secret to Khalid that they wished to join with the Muslims. They asked him when and how they should declare their change of heart. Khalid said that, if they were sincere, they should leave the Christians and must do so at their own discretion. Khalid was of the opinion that the Christians, with or without their Arab auxiliaries, were in a weak state and would collapse if attacked. However, Khalid was not in senior command. Abu 'Ubayda, who was, chose to wait. He ordered the Muslim troops to move to the attack as the reinforcements began to arrive from Kufa. The Jaziris' Arab allies deserted them, even as the Muslims launched their attack, and they were defeated easily and fled in disorder.

In the same year, 17 AH, the Muslims carried through a more deliberate campaign in Jazira. An army of 5,000 was sent out from Iraq under the command of 'Iyad b. Ghanam against the city of Riha. After its capitulation on terms of the *jizya*, 'Iyad proceeded to take control of the whole province in a matter of days, meeting only nominal resistance.

The conquest of Khuzistan

The Muslim stronghold of Basra was vulnerable to attack from Ahwaz (Hurmuz-Shahr), the nearest major city in the contiguous Persian province of Khuzistan. To protect Basra, its governor, Mughira b. Shu'ba, launched a campaign at the beginning of 17 AH against Ahwaz. The chief of Ahwaz sued for peace, obtained it on promise of annual payment of a small sum, and the Muslims withdrew. Mughira had no authority to proceed further: indeed, 'Umar had sent explicit instructions that the Muslims should be content to consolidate the plains of Iraq, not cross either the Zagros Mountains or the Gulf into the Persian heartlands.

Later in the same year, Mughira (whom 'Umar had appointed in 15 AH) was called back to Madina and replaced as governor of Basra by Abu Musa Ash'ari. The chief of Ahwaz took this opportunity to renege on his promise to pay the sum he had agreed. Abu Musa then laid siege to Ahwaz. The Persians fought with wonderful courage and determination but were eventually defeated. The Muslims captured thousands of prisoners and made them slaves but, on the direct order of 'Umar, set them free again.

After Ahwaz, Abu Musa proceeded to besiege Manadhar, a strongly fortified city. Unable to overcome the Persians' resistance

easily, he marched on to Sus with some of his troops, leaving
the rest to continue the siege of Manadhar. But at Sus also he
found the Persians determined to resist to the end. Only when
the citizens were on the edge of starvation did the city's governor
offer to surrender if Abu Musa would spare the lives of a hundred
persons named by him. Abu Musa accepted these terms but,
since the governor had not named himself, had him beheaded.
This high-handed conduct had the immediate consequence that
the next city Abu Musa besieged, Ramharz, surrendered quickly,
obtaining peace from him in exchange for an annual tribute of
800,000 dirhams, a massive sum. But the more important
consequence was that the Persians throughout what remained
of their empire were profoundly incensed against the Arabs. Their
anger, mixed with wounded national pride, made them passionate
in appeals to Yazdgird, now residing at Qom, to prevent the loss
of Khuzistan.

One of those who called upon Yazdgird was Hurmuzan, a
respected noble of high lineage and great influence. He offered
to turn back the tide of defeat if Yazdgird would make him governor
of the provinces of Fars and Ahwaz. Having got this concession,
Hurmuzan made his way to Shustar, the capital city of Khuzistan,
repaired and strengthened its defences, and vigorously set about
the task of gathering and motivating a large army. 'Umar appears
to have been reluctant to send the reinforcements Abu Musa
needed. He first ordered 'Ammar b. Yasir (who had replaced Sa'd
b. Abi Waqqas as governor in Kufa) to dispatch 1,000 men, and
then ordered 'Ammar himself to follow at the head of half the
forces stationed at Kufa. Abu Musa was further strengthened with
the arrival of a large army from Jalula.

Abu Musa then marched on Shustar. He appointed the famous
Companion Anas b. Malik to the command of the cavalry, gave
the right flank to Anas's brother Bara', and the left to the Ansari,
Bara' b. Azib. Hurmuzan, confident of his superiority in numbers,
elected rashly to attack the Muslims. He himself fought gallantly
and slew, among others, two of the Muslims' commanders—Bara'

b. Malik and Bara' b. Azib. In general, however, the Persians did not match the ardour of the Muslims and were defeated. Hurmuzan was forced to retreat to the fortifications of Shustar. There he might have held out if the city's defences had not been betrayed to the Muslims by a Persian deserter. A small force of Muslims was able to penetrate the fortifications by means of an underground waterway and threw the gates open to the main army. With the capture of its capital city, the conquest of the rest of Khuzistan proved uneventful for the Muslims.

Hurmuzan himself evaded capture. He climbed a high citadel with a sheaf of a hundred arrows and secured himself in it. From there he threatened to inflict many casualties on the Muslims unless, on surrendering, he was taken to the Caliph in person, who alone should decide his fate. Abu Musa accepted this condition and sent the Persian general under guard to Madina.

Hurmuzan, though a prisoner, made his entry to Madina in the most brilliant Persian attire. He must have expected to see 'Umar, now one of the world's most powerful rulers, seated upon a grand throne amidst a splendid court. In fact he found 'Umar seated upon the ground (not then paved) of the courtyard of the Mosque. One can easily imagine the impression this picture of Islamic egalitarianism and humility must have made upon Hurmuzan. 'Umar was not minded to be lenient, but listened to what Hurmuzan had to say. The latter asked for a glass of water but hesitated to drink. 'Umar assured him that he would not be slain until he had drunk the water. Hurmuzan promptly overturned the glass and claimed that, by 'Umar's word, he could not now be slain. 'Umar was baffled by this ruse. Hurmuzan then declared his conversion to Islam claiming to have resorted to the ruse so that, his life being safe, people would not accuse him of becoming Muslim to avoid death. The Caliph accepted this claim and permitted the Persian hero to reside in Madina and granted him an annuity to enable him to do so. Hurmuzan proved a useful source of information and was often consulted by 'Umar during later campaigns in Persia.

The invasion of Fars

In 17 AH, seeking to outdo the military triumph of Sa'd b. Abi
Waqqas at Qadisiya, the governor of Bahrayn, 'Ala' b. al-Hadrami,
landed a force by sea in the Persian province of Fars. This expedition
was not authorized by 'Umar, who, as we noted, disapproved any
expansion of the territory under Muslim rule beyond Iraq. When
'Umar learnt of the invasion of Fars he wrote a letter of severe
reprimand to 'Ala'.

The force sent out by 'Ala' under the command of Khalid
b. Mundhir found themselves vastly outnumbered, and were soon
cut off from their ships. They were then obliged to fight a desperate
battle, during which the Persians successfully destroyed the ships.
Khalid b. Mundhir eventually won the battle on the field, but
at the cost of so many Muslims killed that there was no possibility
of continuing with the invasion. On the contrary, he was obliged
to attempt an overland escape to safety in Basra. 'Umar sent a
relief force which met up with the remnants of Khalid's army and,
after a fierce battle with the Persians, extricated them from Fars
and withdrew to Basra.

Nihawand: the 'victory of victories'

The conquest of Khuzistan convinced the Persian Emperor that
the Arabs would not be content with their gains in Iraq and Jazira.
He accordingly sent criers to the nearest and furthest provinces
under his rule—Tabaristan, Jurjan, Damawand, Rayy (later the
site of Tehran), Ispahan, Hamdan, Khurasan and Sind—to con-
tribute men and *matériel* for a force sufficient to expel the Arabs
altogether from his empire. A huge army was thus assembled at
Qom and then sent forward to Nihawand, under the command
of Mardan Shah, the victor of the battle of the Bridge.

The scale of these preparations of course became known to
the governor of Iraq in Kufa. 'Ammar b. Yasir notified 'Umar, who
read out his letter in the Mosque and awaited the counsel of the
assembled Muslims. Though some took the view that all Muslim

forces in Syria and Iraq should be mobilized and dispatched with the Caliph in personal command, it was 'Ali's counsel that prevailed. He pointed out that mobilizing all the forces would expose Syria to re-conquest by the Romans. He recommended, instead, that only one-third of available forces should be sent to face the Persians and that 'Umar should not leave Madina.

'Umar appointed Nu'man b. Maqran as commander-in-chief, with other famous Companions to serve and counsel him (among them were Hudhayfa b. al-Yaman, 'Abdullah the Caliph's son, Jarir Bahli, Mughira b. Shu'ba and 'Amr b. Ma'di Karab). The army marched from Kufa and encamped a few miles from Nihawand where they faced a force that out-numbered them three to one.

To impede cavalry movement against them, the Persians had strewn the approaches to their camp with spikes and thornwood. This was a device the Muslims had already encountered at Jalula. Nu'man invited suggestions for how to deal with it. The battle plan agreed upon remembered a tactic used by Khalid b. al-Walid at the battle of Fihl. A convincingly large body of Muslims were to attempt a direct assault on the enemy camp and, feigning defeat, draw the Persians out toward the Muslims' prepared positions.

Longing for a victory, the Persians were only too eager to pursue the Muslims who appeared to fall back before them. They came within range of a Muslim counter-attack, but Nu'man would not give the order for it to begin. In literal adherence to the example of the Prophet, he was waiting for the sun to pass the meridian. Scores of Muslims in the forward positions were killed but none panicked or broke ranks to commence an assault that had not yet been ordered. When Nu'man finally gave the order, the Muslims hurled themselves at the Persians with an irresistible fury. It is recorded that horses slithered in the gore. Nu'man's horse was among those that fell and he was fearfully mangled while on the ground. His brother, Nu'aym, took the commander's horse and put on his distinctive white cap and mantle so that scarcely anyone knew Nu'man had fallen. When a soldier stopped beside Nu'man to minister to him, he ordered the soldier back to the fight. The carnage continued until nightfall—as many as 30,000 Persians

were killed before they quit the field. After the battle had quietened
down around the dying Muslim commander, he asked a man near
to him what the outcome had been. Hearing that the Muslims
had gained victory, Nu'man gave thanks to God and commanded
that the news be relayed at once to 'Umar.

The remnants of the great Persian army regrouped near to
Hamadan, where the pursuing Muslims defeated them utterly. After
Nihawand, called by Muslim historians the 'victory of victories',
the Persians were never again able to mount a centrally organized
campaign against the Muslims. Their Emperor now entered upon
the final phase of his sad history as the 'King of kings'. At Nihawand,
Hudhayfa b. al-Yaman, the new commander-in-chief, came into
possession of a fabulous horde of jewels collected by Khosrau II.
This treasure was sent intact to Madina, only to be sent back
by the Caliph with the instruction that the precious stones should
be sold and the proceeds distributed to the troops.

Some time after the 'victory of victories', 'Umar addressed
to his council the question: Why were the Persians so determined
to fight against the Muslims? Excepting the unauthorized invasion
of Fars, the Muslims had not ventured to threaten the Persians
in their own lands. On the contrary, the Caliph had publicly said:
'Would that a mountain of fire intervened between us and the
Persians so that they could neither attack us nor we make inroads
into their territory' (Ibn al-Athir, Kamil, 2:538). 'Umar was advised
that the Persian nobles and landowners would never desist from
raising armies against the Muslims while they still cherished the
dream that their ancient empire could be restored. Nor could they
relinquish that dream while there was an emperor who could focus
their loyalty and, at least in theory, gather once again a new imperial
army.

THE CONQUEST OF PERSIA

'Umar accordingly authorized a general invasion of all the dominions
of the Persian empire. The invasion began in 21 AH and was largely,
though not entirely, completed during his caliphate. He prepared

a standard for each province to be subdued and handed it to the man appointed to command the force that would subdue it. 'Umar's commanders sought the easiest route to ensuring a peace favourable to the Muslims. Thus, they did not always attempt outright conquest but often chose, instead, with permission from Madina, to confirm the existing Persian chiefs under the general authority of the Muslims, together with a binding commitment that these chiefs would not raise armies against the Muslims. Inevitably, agreements entered into were sometimes broken by the Persians when they supposed that the tide of war had turned against the Muslims. Conquered cities and districts had then to be 're-conquered'. That is one reason why the sources are sometimes at variance on the dates of battles and the names of the commanders who fought them.

Ispahan and the region called Iraq-Ajam came under secure Muslim authority in the first year of the campaign. From Rayy the Muslims moved into Azerbaijan, which was subdued (twice) in the following year (22 AH). The districts of Jurjan and Dehistan in the province of Tabaristan were won by negotiation rather than battle, the province as a whole being conquered during the caliphate of 'Uthman b. Affan. In the same year, the Muslims advanced from Azerbaijan into Armenia. There, the Magian chief of Bab, claiming to despise the Armenians he governed, surrendered to the Muslims and his troops fought with the Muslim forces that moved on to take Qan on the Aran frontier. The campaigns against Balkh, the capital of Khizar, and Tiflis and the al-Lan Mountains, were only carried through during the caliphate of 'Uthman. The principalities of Kirman, Sistan and Makran (a significant portion of modern Baluchistan) were captured in 23 AH, the last after a particularly fierce battle against Rasal, the local king, who fought heroically at the head of a considerable force including an elephant corps. Some of the elephants, along with news of the victory, were sent to 'Umar in Madina. In his response 'Umar issued a specific order that the campaign should proceed no further. (According to one historian, however, a number of expeditions were launched into the low-lying parts of Daybal and Thana: this would mean that Muslims penetrated to Sind (India) during the caliphate of 'Umar.)

Fars

We referred to the unauthorized invasion of Fars in 17 AH, and the subsequent Muslim withdrawal. However, after Nihawand and 'Umar's decision to subdue Persia, several expeditions were launched against Fars which captured, in close sequence, Sabur, Ardshir, Toj, and Istakhr. Not surprisingly, as this province was the original homeland of the Persians and birthplace of their language, they rebelled and threw off Muslim rule. In 23 AH, the then governor of Bahrayn, 'Uthman b. Abi al-'As, dispatched a large force under the command of his brother Hakam to re-assert Muslim control. Hakam first captured the island of Abarkawan, and then Toj, where he halted, caused mosques to be constructed and settled many Arab families. Using Toj as a base, he sent out expeditions that, slice by slice, added and secured territories from the adjoining districts. The Persian ruler in Fars was eventually forced to field an army which Hakam confronted and defeated at Qamshahr. 'Uthman himself now took the field and sent separate divisions against all the major cities of Fars.

Khurasan: the final defeat of the Persian Emperor

As the Muslim forces advanced, Yazdgird and his imperial court retreated. When (in 22 AH) Ahnaf b. Qays invaded the border principality of Khurasan, the Emperor removed from Marw-Shah-jahan to Marw-Rud. Ahnaf took Marw-Shahjahan, then marched on Marw-Rud. Yazdgird again retreated, now to Balkh, from where he sent out pleas of help to, among others, the Khan of the so-called 'Western' Tartars and the Emperor of China. Substantial reinforcements arrived in the region for the Muslims, but none came for the Persians. At the head of the fresh troops from Kufa, Ahnaf marched to Balkh and captured it. Yazdgird escaped across the river which divided his former empire from the domains of the Chinese Emperor. The latter welcomed him but offered little practical help except perhaps to urge the Tartars to assist him. With an army of Tartars behind him, the ill-fated Yazdgird crossed back into Khurasan. In response, Ahnaf withdrew toward Marw-Rud, where he encamped. Yazdgird detached himself from the main Tartar army and advanced separately on Marw-Shahjahan. Ahnaf, not wishing to engage the Persian–Tartar forces on the plain, moved his troops to safer positions on high ground with the mountains behind them. Each army waited for the other to make the first move. Persian warriors would come out, fully armed, on to the field between the encamped forces, but no Muslims were sent out to challenge them. The Tartars would likewise come out for single combat, accompanied by martial music. On one of these occasions, the Muslim commander himself rode out to take on the Tartar champion and, after a long fight, killed him. Two other Tartar warriors in succession met the same fate. The Khan of the Tartars, having witnessed this scene, and perhaps also influenced by the absence of Yazdgird, decided that this was not his people's war and abandoned the Persians.

Yazdgird now despaired. He collected his personal treasures and resolved to seek refuge with the Tartars. His courtiers, incensed by the collapse in their prospects of ever regaining their lost territories and prestige, turned upon him and despoiled him of his treasures. The wretched 'King of kings' escaped with only his life and the apparel on his back to refuge in Farghana, the capital of the Khan. His death occurred after the end of 'Umar's caliphate.

News of final victory was relayed to Madina and the Caliph announced it in person to the Muslims assembled in the Mosque for that purpose. He said: 'The empire of the Magians has this day passed away. They no longer own even a hand's breadth of the territory of their cities that can pose a threat' (Ibn Athir, *Kamil*, 3:37).

THE CONQUEST OF EGYPT

'Umar was not in favour of an attempt to conquer Egypt, an idea put to him by 'Amr b. al-'As, probably when the Caliph was in Jerusalem to accept the surrender of that city. On account of the province's economic importance to the Romans, Egypt would not be easily taken from them; moreover, there was no significant Arab population that might be expected to welcome the Muslims and their faith and assist them in holding the territory, if indeed it could be captured; also, the Roman forces in Egypt did not present any immediate danger to the Muslims' rule in Syria.

The capture of Qaysaria

What may have inclined the Caliph to change his decision is the difficulty the Muslims experienced in taking the coastal fortress of Qaysaria (Caesarea): they did not have the artillery to penetrate its walls, and its inhabitants and garrison were regularly supplied by the Roman fleet operating out of Egypt's capital city, Alexandria— the Muslims of course did not have a navy at this time. The fortress was first besieged in 13 AH by 'Amr b. al-'As. It held out even after Yarmuk and the fall of Jerusalem, when the Roman garrisons were cleared throughout Syria. After the death of Abu 'Ubayda, 'Umar instructed Yazid b. Abi Sufyan to besiege Qaysaria, which he did with 17,000 troops. Yazid was taken ill during this campaign and returned to Damascus, where he died. His brother Mu'awiya took over the siege and prosecuted it vigorously. But, despite victories over Roman troops who sallied out of the fortress from time to time, the city continued to hold out. Eventually, a Jew named Yusuf came to Mu'awiya and disclosed to him an underground passage that led behind the fortifications. A detachment of Muslims gained access by this route and opened the gates of the city, which was then successfully stormed in 19 AH, nearly two years after the capture of Jerusalem.

The decision to invade Egypt

Before his conversion to Islam, 'Amr b. al-'As had on many occasions visited Egypt as a trader and so knew the land well. During 'Umar's stay in Syria after the plague of Amwas, 'Amr persuaded the reluctant Caliph to endorse an expedition. 'Amr was put at the head of 4,000 troops with the instruction to expect a letter from 'Umar, who was still considering his decision. If the Caliph's letter reached him before he had crossed into Egypt, he was to return. In the event, the letter reached 'Amr at either 'Arish or (according to another source) at Rafah: in either case, 'Amr was already in Egypt and therefore did not feel he had to turn back.

The capture of Farama and Fustat

'Amr proceeded along the coast to Farama where he faced a substantial Roman garrison. This ancient port (Pelusium) was then a populous city and famous as the burial place of Galen. 'Amr worked away at the Roman garrison for a whole month, wearing them down by attrition, until a fierce, final battle settled the issue. From there, 'Amr marched in almost a straight line to the great imperial fortress at the apex of the triangle formed by the Nile delta. This fortress, later the site of Fustat, was the seat of government for this part of Egypt. It had unusually massive walls and could be, indeed was, supplied by river from the Mediterranean. Upon its capture depended control of the delta province of Misr and important cities down the Nile. En route to the fortress, 'Amr fought successful engagements against the garrisons at Balbis and Umm Danin and captured these places. The Romans, we may note, got little support from the local Egyptians (Copts) whose doctrines differed from those of the Greek Orthodox Church supported by the Roman (Byzantine) emperor. For all that, it was impossible with the force at 'Amr's disposal successfully to besiege a fortress whose supply lines he could not cut and whose impenetrable walls and parapets could rain down missiles on his men. 'Amr therefore settled his troops in entrenched positions and sent to Madina for reinforcements.

'Umar dispatched a force of 10,000, pointing out in the accompanying letter that four of the captains of this force were equivalent in quality to a thousand horsemen. The four were: Zubayr b. al-Awwam, 'Ubada b. al-Samit, Miqdad b. 'Umar, and Maslama b. Mukhallad. 'Amr handed over conduct of the siege operations to Zubayr, who organized the disposition of cavalry, infantry, and artillery around the fortress. However, the catapults available to the Muslims made little impression on the Romans' fortifications. For seven months, the siege continued in this way until Zubayr finally determined that he would personally scale the walls and, if need be, give his life in the endeavour to serve Islam. Accompanied by a few equally committed comrades, Zubayr then scaled the wall using rope ladders. On attaining the parapet, this handful of Muslims shouted *Allahu akbar*, a signal for the main force outside to do the same. The sheer volume and enthusiasm of the shout may have convinced the Romans that somehow the Muslims had gained access. However it may be, Zubayr and the others managed to climb down to the gates and open them, allowing the Muslim army to pour in. The Roman governor, referred to in the Arabic sources as al-Maqawqas, recognizing the advantage the Muslims had secured, surrendered and negotiated a treaty of peace.

According to its terms, the Romans were to abandon the whole of Egypt, but the treaty was conditional on ratification by the Emperor in Constantinople. The ageing Heraclius refused outright to ratify the surrender of Egypt; rather, he dispatched substantial reinforcements to Alexandria to assert Roman authority and, where possible, to recover territory lost to the Arabs. The Muslims had therefore to fight on.

The incident of the tent

'Amr remained for some while in the great fortress the Muslims had just conquered, awaiting permission from the Caliph in Madina to proceed to Alexandria. When permission came and it was time to strike camp, a pigeon's nest was discovered in the commander's tent. 'Amr is reported to have ordered the tent to be left standing so as not to inconvenience the bird. The Arabic for tent, *fustat*, inspired the name of the city founded by 'Amr at this site after his return from the conquest of Alexandria.

The capture of Alexandria (21 AH)

Al-Maqawqas returned directly to Alexandria, after the death of Heraclius, as Roman governor of Egypt. He wanted, on behalf of the Copts, to negotiate with the Muslims favourable terms for the surrender of the province. However, he was opposed in this policy by the Romans in Egypt and by one of the several factions contending for power and legitimacy in Constantinople. He had to bide his time and go along with the expectations of the Roman garrison.

'Amr was confronted by Roman troops at several points on his march to the city of Alexander and defeated them, often assisted in crossing and re-crossing the Nile by the local Copts. From Alexandria a substantial Roman force, comprising the fresh troops from Constantinople and including auxiliary units of Copts, was sent out to prevent the Muslims' further advance to the Egyptian capital. The opposing armies met at Kariun, where, after some days of small engagements, the Romans' formations were destroyed by a fierce charge by the Muslims. All further resistance was hereafter focused in the city-fortress itself, which the Muslims now besieged. It is explicitly recorded in the sources that the local population provided supplies to the Muslim troops during the siege and assisted them by repairing bridges and roads that they needed to use. It is possible that al-Maqawqas conducted secret negotiations with 'Amr, that is, without the knowledge of the Roman garrison commander.

Alexandria, which had been founded a thousand years earlier, was the Roman empire's second city. It had, by the standards of the time, a huge population, great palaces, many public buildings and important churches, and, in its harbour, the famous lighthouse, boasted as one of the seven wonders of the world. In addition to the high, massive double walls and towers enclosing it, the city had the Mediterranean on one side, and Lake Mareotis and many canals on the other, leaving only a narrow front against which defence could be concentrated effectively. It is well to reflect upon the ancient glory of the place and the scale of the military task the Muslims faced in taking on Alexandria, and what defeat or victory in the enterprise meant for both sides.

There was little prospect of the Muslims gaining entry and, if the political situation had been stable in Constantinople, no doubt the garrison might have been content to wait within their defences indefinitely. However, the maintenance of morale was a vital issue and the Romans chose from time to time to sally out and engage the Muslims. They were invariably pushed back, but the Muslims for their part failed to breach the city's defences. The siege continued in this way for several months.

'Umar, anxious for the issue to be resolved, wrote to 'Amr b. al-'As: 'Perhaps the luxuries of Egypt have influenced you to become indolent lovers of ease like the Christians, for otherwise victory could not have been so long delayed. I urge you, on receiving this letter, to assemble the men and deliver to them a sermon on *jihad*. After that, command an assault with officers leading the charge and the troops behind, and all moving with one accord' (Maqrizi, 1:165).

'Amr delivered the sermon, stirring the men to the highest pitch of enthusiasm. Then he publicly named 'Ubada b. al-Samit, a Companion of the Prophet of long standing, as commander-in-chief, and confirmed Zubayr b. al-Awwam and Maslama b. Mukhallad as commanders of the vanguard. In this frame of mind, united and passionate for victory, the Muslims bore down on Alexandria and took the city, as it were by sheer force of morale and, quite possibly, some degree of support from the Copts.

As noted earlier, the Copts, whom al-Maqawqas claimed to represent, though he was the representative of the Roman emperor, were disposed to settle terms of peace with the Muslims. However, there were Roman garrisons elsewhere in Egypt and, after the capture of Alexandria, 'Amr dispatched troops in all directions to secure their surrender, notably at Tanis and Dimiyat (Damietta).

Celebration of the victory

'Amr b. al-'As sent news of the capture of Alexandria to 'Umar by direct messenger. The messenger, Mu'awiya b. Khudajj, reached

Madina just after noon and, not wishing to disturb the Caliph at that time of day, proceeded to the Mosque. One of the Caliph's servants guessed that Mu'awiya was a traveller and asked from where he had come. On hearing the answer, the servant hastened to tell 'Umar who ordered her to go to the Mosque and send the traveller to him. So impatient was 'Umar to hear the news that he dressed to go to the Mosque rather than wait for the messenger to come to him. The two met as 'Umar was about to leave. Mu'awiya gave his most welcome message and the Caliph thanked God.

After the news had been made public in the Mosque, 'Umar invited Mu'awiya back to his house for refreshments. There he asked him: 'Why did you not come to me straight away?' Mu'awiya said: 'I thought, as it was the hour of rest, you might be asleep.' 'Umar replied to this: 'I am sorry you have such a poor opinion of me. Who would bear the burden of caliphate if I were to sleep during the day?' (Maqrizi 1:166). Then, the servant brought in the food for the Caliph's guest: it consisted of bread and olive oil. Thus did the world's most powerful ruler, as 'Umar then was, celebrate one of the greatest victories of his caliphate.

The assassination of 'Umar

At the battle of Nihawand, a Persian named Firoz was taken prisoner and fell to the lot of Mughira b. Shu'ba. Mughira brought this Firoz to Madina, where he earned a living as a carpenter, painter, and ironsmith. Being Mughira's slave, Firoz was obliged to make a daily payment to his master from his earnings. The Persian was aware that, under Islamic law as then enforced, he could bring a grievance against his master if he felt that he was being overburdened. On the 25th Dhu l-Hijjah, 23 AH, Firoz brought his complaint before the Caliph. 'Umar asked him how much he had to pay his master and learnt that the amount was two dirhams daily. 'Umar then asked how he earned his living and, on being told, gave the judgement that these occupations were very well paid and that, therefore, he, Firoz, was not overburdened by his master.

On the very next day, Firoz made his way to the front rank of the worshippers assembled in the Mosque for the prayer at dawn. As 'Umar committed his attention to prayer with *Allahu akbar*, and the congregation behind him did the same, Firoz stepped forward and stabbed 'Umar six times. The Caliph fell and motioned 'Abd al-Rahman b. 'Awf to resume and conclude the service of prayer. Meantime, Firoz managed to take his own life before he could be overpowered.

After the end of the prayer, 'Umar was carried to his house. He asked who had stabbed him and thanked God that it had not been a Muslim. A physician attended him and served him some milk and a cordial made from dates. Both drinks flowed directly out of his wounds. The people then realized that 'Umar would not survive and asked him to nominate his successor.

The Caliph called for his son 'Abdullah and sent him to greet 'A'isha and beg from her, on his behalf, permission to be buried alongside the Prophet. 'Abdullah went to 'A'isha and found her weeping. He conveyed his father's greetings and his request. She said: 'I had a mind to reserve that place for myself. But this day I shall accord to 'Umar precedence over myself.' 'Abdullah returned to his father, who asked: 'What news do you bring me, my son?' 'That which is calculated to give you contentment.' Then 'Umar said: 'It was the greatest wish of my life' (Ibn Sa'd, 3:338).

Before this occasion, the Companions had often urged 'Umar to reflect upon the necessity of nominating his successor. He was of course fully aware of the importance and urgency of doing so. But he was unable to determine who out of the possible candidates was best suited to bear the responsibility of the caliphate at that time. The six most likely persons were: 'Ali, 'Uthman, Zubayr, Talha, Sa'd b. Abi Waqqas and 'Abd al-Rahman b. 'Awf. However, in each of these men he detected some lack that caused him to have misgivings.

In spite of the pain from his wounds, 'Umar continued to apply himself to some resolution of this problem. In the end, he recommended that whoever of the six commanded the largest support should be elected. He added most emphatically this counsel:

'Whoever is elected caliph, I charge him to respect to the utmost the rights and privileges of these five sections of the people: the Muhajirun, the Ansar, the Bedouins, those Arabs who have migrated to foreign cities, and the *dhimmis* [the Christians, the Jews, and the Magians] who are the subjects of Islamic rule.' He proceeded to enumerate the rights of each group. Of the *dhimmis*, he said: 'It is my parting behest to the caliph that he should pay proper regard to the Muslims' responsibilities to God and His Messenger, that is, the contract entered into with the *dhimmis* should be respected, their enemies should be repelled and they should not be subjected to that which is beyond their endurance' (Ibn Sa'd 3:339).

Having settled his public duty, 'Umar turned to his private affairs. He again called his son, 'Abdullah, and asked what his ('Umar's) debts were. They stood at 86,000 dirhams. He asked that this debt be settled from his personal wealth as far as possible; the liability that remained should be offered to the clan of 'Adiy to clear; if they could not, then to the tribe of Quraysh as a whole, but no one else should be asked. In the event, a house belonging to the clan of 'Adiy, situated near the Mosque in Makka between the two famous gates, Bab al-Salam and Bab al-Rahma, was purchased by Mu'awiya b. Abi Sufyan, and the Caliph's debt was cleared from the proceeds.

'Umar died three days after he had been stabbed and was buried on Saturday, 1st Muharram. His caliphate had lasted ten years, six months and four days. His body was lowered into his grave by 'Abd al-Rahman b. 'Awf, and the greatest ruler the Muslims were ever to have was hidden in the dust for good: *inna li-llahi wa inna ilay-hi raji'un*—it is to God we belong and it is to Him we are returning.

4

The Cause of Victory

During the first half of 'Umar's caliphate, most of Iraq and the Roman province of Syria came under secure Muslim rule. In the second half, to these were added most of the dominions of the Persian empire and the Roman province of Egypt. To appreciate the magnitude of this achievement, it is worthwhile reviewing briefly the general situation of the peoples of the Arab Peninsula *vis-à-vis* the Persian and Roman empires on its borders.

The power of the Sassanid dynasty that ruled most of the former Parthian dominions was greatly weakened by the westward migration, in the fifth century, of the so-called 'White Huns'. In consequence, the Byzantine Romans regained control of the Syria–Mesopotamia–Asia Minor territories that had long been contested between Romans and Parthians. However, in the early sixth century, under Khosrau I, the Sassanids defeated the Romans decisively and took new territories as far north as the Caucasus Mountains. Khosrau II extended the Persian empire westward into Egypt during a period of turmoil in the Byzantine court when the Romans also lost their Balkan provinces. Then, re-invigorated under the Emperor Heraclius, the Romans in a five-year campaign forced the Persians out of Egypt, Palestine and Syria, and most of Upper Mesopotamia:

it is this victory of Romans over Persians that is alluded to in the Qur'an (30.1).

Thus, at the epoch we are considering, it would be hard to describe military energy or capacity as terminally low among either the Romans or the Persians: compared to the Arabs, both these states were overwhelmingly powerful. The Arabs living within the Roman territories of Syria, Jordan, and Palestine, as well as the Arab tribes of the border regions, were mostly, though not wholly, Christian, and identified with their Roman co-religionists. Their tribal chiefs (sometimes aggrandized with the title of king) functioned as governors under Roman protectorate. At the opposite, southern, end of the Peninsula, the Arabs of Najran and Yemen (who likewise included some Christians) were under the rule of governors appointed by the Persian court. Bahrayn and the adjacent coastal area were also under the control of the Persians, though the degree of control varied. Neither the western region of the Hijaz nor the central desert plains of Najd were of direct interest to either Romans or Persians. The Arab tribes here were almost wholly polytheist until the advent of Islam, excepting the few, influential Jewish tribes whose settlements in Yathrib (Madina) and Khaybar were mentioned in the first chapter. There were long-standing contacts, sustained by trade and other factors, between the polytheist Arabs, the Christian Arabs who owed allegiance to the Romans, and the Arabs of the eastern and southern coastal areas who owed allegiance to the Persians. Where there was so much contact, there was necessarily also the potential for considerable influence.

Southern Iraq and the adjacent region of Arabia proper had only rarely fallen under Roman occupation: for centuries past it had been dominated by the Persians. The northern Arab tribes, as well as the Arabs settled in Mesopotamia, were weakened by feuding and relative cultural backwardness. Nevertheless, they had sufficient feeling of national solidarity to unite from time to time and strive for independence. Their success depended less upon themselves than on the determination of the Persians to hold on to suzerainty. Whenever disorder prevailed in the Persian court, the Arabs rebelled. There was an independent Arab kingdom of Iraq with its capital at Hira, which even extended its power southwards, but it could not endure. For, as had happened many times before, when authority in the Persian court was stable, the Persians re-established their overlordship and did so with a display of brutality remembered (and meant to be remembered) long afterwards.

How, then, were the Arabs able not only to rebel against the Persians but to conquer the whole of Iraq and to do so almost concurrently with their conquests into Syria to the north? They could not so abruptly have acquired a nationalist fervour sufficient to override their tribal divisions. Even if they had, they still remained, in organization, numbers, equipment, and in every other respect, as they had been for centuries, greatly inferior to the Persians and Romans. Nor can the Arabs' achievement be attributed to momentum: they did not, as it were, seize the opportunity to win one great battle, and having won it go on winning unstoppably. On the contrary, they experienced shattering reverses as well as dramatic victories: there were many opportunities for the powers they challenged to muster their superior forces and defeat them. Nor, as we have seen, were the engagements all of one kind— the Arabs waged long, pitched battles as well as guerrilla raids, defensive as well as offensive campaigns, and on diverse terrains in different climates.

It is easy to grasp how the pagan Arabs may have dreamed of freeing their territories from foreign rule, of avenging centuries of defeat and humiliation. But they surely cannot have imagined conquering those same foreign rulers' territories and ruling in their place as overlords. The commonly offered explanations—that the Arabs were driven to expansion by drought and famine, or by the desire for plunder, or by the opportunity presented by the weakness of the Romans and the Persians at the time—are unsatisfactory. Situations such as extreme drought and the desire for plunder must have existed before. Similarly, Romans and Persians had weakened each other in long wars before, but the

Arabs had never managed to hold on to any victory over either. What had changed was that these Arabs were now led by an elite of men committed to the rule of Islam. That commitment gave them the authority as Muslims to rule over themselves (that is, to unite as a people) and then to rule over non-Arabs and non-Muslims, and do so according to a Scripture in whose Divine origin they had absolute conviction. The failure to secure a victory that brought and held the conquered territories within the rule of Islam would surely have meant that the Arabs missed their hour to become a civilized, civilizing power in the world. Their acceptance of Islam was a declaration that they had rejected their former *jahiliyya* (barbarism). The conquests are best understood as the Muslims' effort (*jihad*) to express and evolve, on a grand scale, the meaning of that rejection of *jahiliyya*.

The decisive factors in the Muslims' success on the battlefield were superior morale and superior command. Their campaigns were not undertaken in a mad rush for spoils nor in a trance of religious fervour. Probably defensive or pre-emptive in the first instance, by the time 'Umar became Caliph the campaigns into the contiguous lands of Syria and Iraq were a clear and steady policy with definite objectives. The Muslims moved into those provinces under Roman or Persian control where there was already a significant population of Arabs who could be expected to respond positively to the Qur'an, the Revelation of God's Will in Arabic.

That Revelation, together with the teaching and example of the Prophet that accompanied and embodied it (the Sunna), initiated a new order that touched the everyday life and self-image of every individual who accepted it. The disciplines of prayer and fasting, of alms tax and pilgrimage, were obligations upon all Muslims equally; the 'best' differed only in the quality of commitment they brought to fulfilling those obligations and the quality of their understanding of their meaning. When Islam was taken to the Arabs who had not yet accepted it, it was seen by them as a way of life shared by their fellow Arabs, all equally, and not as a body of doctrines or mysteries that only a privileged few could understand and explain. The dignity of being a Muslim, and the pride the believers took in that dignity, was at the same time morally ennobling and socially levelling. In every negotiation with their enemies, the Muslim envoys stressed with great pride that their ruler was but one of themselves, subject to the same law. Power derived from moral authority which was not inherently mysterious nor, since Abu Bakr and not 'Ali had succeeded as Caliph, inaccessible because hereditary. In principle, any Muslim could claim a share in that authority who could argue competently from the Qur'an and Sunna, or from general custom and practice not amended by either. The Muslims fought with a passionate need to win because enough of them understood that the rule of Islam could bring a more just order than either they or the peoples they conquered had imagined before.

The victories on the battlefield must have counted at that time (for both victors and vanquished) as a strong argument in favour of the new order, particularly in combination with the clarity and inherent appeal of Islamic ideals and the conduct of the elite who tried to embody them. The majority of the conquered peoples were Arabic- or Aramaic-speaking and, under the Muslims of the Peninsula, enjoyed a regime more benign than that of the Romans or Persians. The Muslims when retaking territory they had lost did not carry out punitive reprisals. On the contrary, they appear to have recognized that the local peoples would have had little choice but to reaffirm allegiance to their former overlords. There was no reason, except their commitment to Islam, which prevented the conquering Arabs from behaving in the manner of those whose rule they replaced. But in general they did not. In all the conquests of this period, the Muslims razed no cities, nor did they massacre their inhabitants, lay waste their fields and orchards, or enslave them en masse, as a way of encouraging other cities to surrender quickly. Following 'Umar's decree, lands whose owners had fled or been slain were prohibited to the conquerors. These lands became the property of the state, and their revenues were used for public purposes. Even for slaves, government was lawful: they enjoyed the hope of earning their emancipation and legal rights against their owners which could be enforced—the case of the Persian slave who murdered 'Umar is the best known, not the only, example.

Therefore, when Muslims, alongside or after the armies, migrated to the conquered territories of Iraq, Syria, or Egypt, they were generally welcomed, as was their new faith. During the caliphate of 'Umar, garrison settlements were established which grew into towns and cities, Kufa, Basra, and Fustat being the most important, and the immigrants co-existed, then merged, relatively easily with the local population. And many of the converts to Islam, whether formerly Jewish or Christian or Magian, were settled in these new cities.

The conquests in 'Umar's reign, and their durability, must therefore be attributed to the unifying and inspiring force of Islam in its character as an ideal of just government. No Muslim at that time, nor any since, realized or represented that ideal of just government better than 'Umar. The Muslims he commanded had complete confidence in the integrity of the Caliph's person and his government, certain that in obeying him they served the cause of Islam. To understand how 'Umar was able to inspire such loyalty and trust, we need to understand how he embodied his commitment to Islam in specific measures of government, law, and administration. The conquests were not achieved by religious zeal alone, but also by taking all the necessary steps in the right order and at the right time. In the same way, the unifying authority of Islam was not achieved simply by the Muslims passionately desiring it, but by creative thinking through and resolving of the difficulties they faced in the light of the Qur'an and its embodiment in the Sunna.

Part II

The Reforms

Map 3. *The eastern Mediterranean in the caliphate of 'Umar*

5

Government under 'Umar

Just as the conquests secured Islam territorially, defining for good its geographical heartlands, the reforms 'Umar achieved in Islamic law, government, and administration defined many of its important characteristics as a civilization. As we noted earlier, 'Umar was profoundly attuned to the character and ideals of Islam. With the help of other senior Companions, he was able to direct the talents and energies of the Muslims in ways that they recognized as Islamic and which, therefore, they either supported wholeheartedly or (at worst) had not the heart to oppose.

He believed that the guidance of Qur'an and Sunna sufficed to meet any challenges that would face the Muslims. He believed also in the *reasonableness* of that guidance: its principles and ideals were not a mystery, but could be discussed and understood, explained and applied. From that followed the all-important principle that legitimate authority in Islam could not rest upon any other relationship with that guidance than the ability to understand, explain, and apply it. It could not, for example, rest upon proximity to the Prophet, nor upon ties of family or kinship with him, nor (since Revelation had ceased) upon claims of Divine inspiration.

The quality of 'Umar's understanding of Islam is clearest in his contribution to the sciences of Hadith criticism and *fiqh*, the basis for evolving legal norms and rulings from the Qur'an and

Sunna. This we shall study in a later chapter, after an account of his reforms of government and administration.

Consultative assemblies

'Umar commented upon the accession of Abu Bakr: 'Though it was sudden, God safeguarded us against its unsafe implications (*sharra-ha*)' (Bukhari, 8:540). As Abu Bakr governed for the good of the Muslims as a whole and for the sake of Islam, his rule was widely accepted. Nevertheless, the question of legitimacy continued to concern 'Umar. During his term as Caliph he laboured energetically to evolve procedures that would secure acceptance for the institution of caliphate.

The most important of his reforms was the establishment of a consultative assembly. Every question of moment was referred to this body and no decision taken without free debate and majority consent. Seniority in Islam belonged at that time to two groups among the Arabs, namely the Madinan Ansar or Helpers and the Makkan Muhajirun or Emigrants, who were both represented on the Assembly. Meetings were convened by a public crier and held at the Mosque. When the people had gathered, 'Umar led them in prayer before addressing them from the pulpit on the matter at hand.

For questions of unusual significance, a larger assembly was convened which might sit for several days. On the subject of whether the conquered lands in Iraq and Syria should be divided up among the army as private estates, 'Umar opened debate with this encouragement to free speech: 'I have troubled you to assemble here in order that you might share the burdens placed upon me in respect of the state, for I am only one among yourselves, and I do not desire that you should [merely] follow my wishes' (Abu Yusuf, 25). Among other matters settled in this larger assembly were the pay of soldiers, the organization of the secretariat, major administrative appointments, the freedom to trade accorded to foreigners, the rates and assessment of import duties, and so on. Lesser matters and day-to-day administration were referred by 'Umar to a select group of the Muhajirun who met always in the Prophet's Mosque. They received daily reports from districts and provinces and discussed any details that needed discussion. A famous instance of a subject that was first broached in this Council was whether *jizya* should be levied on the Magians of the conquered Persian territories.

The role of the Caliph

The Assembly's success as a body for discussing, formulating, and enacting policy is due in large part to the talents of the Caliph. 'Umar had been respected even before his conversion to Islam as an accomplished speaker (one who could think and find the right words quickly), an expert in the genealogy of the Arabs, and a skilful negotiator. His training under the Prophet and his commitment to Islam deepened all of these talents. As Caliph, he showed astonishing intellectual powers. He was able to divide his attention between several complex matters of the highest consequence and manage them concurrently, with undiminished concentration and without losing sight of general objectives. He was able to penetrate quickly to the essentials of a situation, guide discussion about it, then reach decisions and put them into effect in almost a single movement of energy. It is hardly surprising that, given also his effective speaking skills and his instinctively authoritative manner, people held him in awe, listened and learned and, after their chance to speak and give counsel, obeyed. Most remarkable of all, perhaps, is 'Umar's grasp of detail alongside grasp of the overall picture.

A small but telling example is the institution of the Islamic calendar. 'Umar was once handed a document on which was written *Sha'ban*, the month, with no indication of the year. 'Umar promptly assembled the senior Companions in order to consult them on the best solution. The majority favoured adopting a calendar in the Persian style. 'Ali is credited with proposing that the era should begin from the day of the Prophet's emigration from Makka to Madina. If this notion had been strictly followed, the calendar would have begun in Rabi' I, two months and eight days after the 1st of Muharram, new year's day among the Arabs by ancient custom. The 1st of Muharram of the year in which the *Hijra* took place was eventually accepted as the starting date. The solution was quick, most easily practicable, and appropriate. Many of the issues the Muslims faced were dealt with in this manner, though some required more debate in order to achieve consensus. Under 'Umar's leadership, there was a momentum to solve actual problems, rather than become involved in hypothetical or abstract issues.

'Umar's capacity to deal successfully with details is due in part to his aversion to procrastination. He advised against letting little tasks accumulate: the result is always too many tasks to deal with and no way of deciding which to start with. Once, while he was speaking at the Mosque in Makka, 'Umar was interrupted by a Christian who complained that he had been charged customs duties twice and gave particulars. 'Umar replied simply 'Customs cannot be charged twice', and resumed his address. Some days later the man came before 'Umar and said that he was the same Christian who had made such and such a complaint. 'Umar told him that he was the same Muslim who had heard and redressed his grievance. In fact, 'Umar had written to the offending customs officer (one Ziyad b. Hadir in Iraq) the same day (Abu Yusuf, 136).

The role of the ordinary subject

The Qur'anic injunction that people should be consulted in decisions affecting them was embodied by 'Umar in several measures. First, he tried to secure the consent of the people to the appointment of officials over them. For example, when provincial revenue officers were needed for Kufa, Basra, and Syria, he asked the people of each province to nominate suitable persons. Their nominees then presented themselves in Madina, where the Caliph duly confirmed their appointment. Second, 'Umar widely and regularly proclaimed the right of individual subjects to air their grievances against any government official. Further, he acted upon popular complaints. For example, 'Umar deposed Sa'd b. Abi Waqqas, an eminent

Companion and the conqueror of Mada'in, from the governorship of Kufa in response to criticisms about his style of government. Third, 'Umar kept himself directly informed of the reputation every senior officer earned in the conduct of his duties and promptly disciplined those who were found at fault.

We shall describe in the next chapter the specific precautions 'Umar took to ensure the competence and propriety of his officers. Here, we must note that all the Caliph's efforts in this regard would have counted for little if he had not himself led by example. He stressed repeatedly that, as regards the Law, he stood on an equal footing with any other individual. He claimed no special privileges or exemptions as caliph. He proclaimed, instead, that his powers were limited and his exercise of them subject to scrutiny and criticism. Regarding public funds, he said: 'I have no greater right on your money [i.e. public funds] than the guardian of an orphan has on that orphan's property. If I am wealthy, I shall not take anything. If I am needy, I shall take for my maintenance according to usage. You people—you have many rights on me which you should demand of me. One of those rights is that I should not collect revenues and spoils of war unlawfully; the second is that the revenues and spoils of war that come into my possession should not be spent unlawfully; another is that I should increase your stipends and protect the frontiers, and that I should not cast you into unnecessary perils' (Abu Yusuf, 117).

Criticism of the Caliph

Freedom of speech in regard to the functions of government is the right of the governed, balanced against their duty to prevent the government from falling into abuses of power. And the government cannot claim that duty of them without granting the corresponding right. 'Umar's conduct shows that he clearly grasped this principle. The temperament of the Arabs at that time could be fiercely individualistic. At its worst, this quality inclined them to anarchy, but at its best it could be a courageous independence of spirit which 'Umar sought to foster. The people were both openly critical when occasion demanded and whole-heartedly supportive of the ruler who permitted them to be so. It was a difficult balance.

Under the rule of 'Uthman and 'Ali, tolerance of free speech became a factor in encouraging civil strife; under 'Umar's leadership, it was a means of strong government. One of the reasons for the general acceptance of his decision to depose Khalid b. al-Walid from military command was that 'Umar had allowed the decision to be challenged. On his tour of Syria, a Muslim criticized him vigorously: 'By God, 'Umar, you have not acted justly. You have dismissed a man whom the Messenger of God himself appointed; you have returned to its sheath the sword that God's Messenger had drawn. And you have disregarded the ties of kinship and envied your cousin.' 'Umar listened to the whole of this and then said: 'Loyalty to your [Muslim] brother has made you angry' (Ibn Athir, *Usd* 1:53).

Encouragement to equality

'Umar's own first loyalty was not to any individual or clan but to Islam. In this respect he had to work against, not with, the instincts and usages of the Arabs, but in doing so he did no more than follow as closely as practicable the Prophet's example. For that reason, the people either supported him willingly or they acquiesced. For example, after the battle of Qadisiya many of the Quraysh nobility and other tribal leaders cherished high expectations. But 'Umar ignored social distinctions altogether and fixed stipends with reference to seniority and merit in service to Islam. Thus, preference was given to those who had been earliest in embracing Islam and/or had distinguished themselves in the early battles, or had been dearer or nearer to the Prophet. If in these respects two individuals were equal, their stipends were equal, even if one was a slave and the other a noble. Usama b. Zayd was given a higher stipend than 'Abdullah, the Caliph's son, who protested that he had not been second to Usama on any occasion. 'Umar explained that the Prophet had loved Usama more than he had loved him.

The consent of the governed

For all the Caliph's political skills, or the correctness of the administration he sought to establish, so vast an area comprising
so many disparate peoples so recently at war with each other could
not have been governed as well as it was without the cooperation
of the overwhelming majority of the governed. That cooperation
was earned by 'Umar's impeccable reputation for integrity and
impartiality in the exercise of power. The people consented to
his rule because they were certain that his decisions were principled, not opportunistic, and they obeyed his officers because he
had appointed them and because, if they were at fault, he disciplined them without deference to their social rank or even to
their former services to Islam. This policy might have provoked
rebellion by the great men whom 'Umar disciplined or, more simply,
did not promote to high office, if 'Umar had not shown that he
exercised the same severity upon himself and his own, and in
pursuit of the same ideals. The importance of setting a good example
at the top explains his implacable severity, indeed harshness of
speech and manner, on a number of occasions.

Ubayy b. Ka'b lodged a suit against 'Umar in the court of
Zayd b. Thabit. When Zayd directed the Caliph to a seat of honour
in the court, 'Umar refused and promptly seated himself beside
the plaintiff. Ubayy, having no proof of his claim, demanded
according to usage that 'Umar take an oath to defend against
the claim. Zayd ventured to suggest that he might waive this right
in view of 'Umar's position as the caliph. But the Caliph reprimanded him, insisting that the judge must observe strict equality.
Notwithstanding Zayd's discomfiture (he had been the Prophet's
amanuensis), the point was too important for 'Umar to lose the
opportunity of making it. When his son Abu Shahma was to be
flogged for drinking wine, 'Umar carried out the punishment with
his own hand and in public. Qadama b. Maz'un, the Caliph's brother-
in-law and a Companion of high rank, was convicted of the
same offence and received the same punishment. Similarly, when
'Abdullah, the son of 'Amr b. al-'As, beat a Copt without just

cause, 'Umar had him beaten by the Copt, and the conqueror of Egypt was required to attend the occasion of his son's punishment.

There was no more striking demonstration of 'Umar's disinterested service than his management of public wealth. For example, in an exchange of courtesies with the Byzantine Emperor, the Caliph's wife, Umm Kulthum, sent the Emperor's wife some vials of perfume which were returned full of gems. 'Umar confiscated the gems for the public treasury on the grounds that the vials had been carried to and from Constantinople by an employee of the state, and compensated his wife for the cost of the perfume. He took from the public treasury only the salary agreed for him in the Assembly. It was fixed (at 'Ali's suggestion) as 'food and clothes of average standard' for himself and his family. Later, it was replaced by the state stipend of 5,000 dirhams granted equally to all the Muslims who had fought at Badr.

Without such strictness, and without public knowledge of it, 'Umar could not have carried his policy of not appointing any men of the Prophet's own clan, the Hashim, to provincial governorships. This policy was in response to the controversy over the *khums* or fifth of the spoils of war (discussed more fully below). 'Umar regarded *khums* as state property. The Hashimis regarded it as a personal, heritable property of the Prophet and, as his direct heirs, claimed it as theirs by right, privately, to dispose of as they wished.

Constitutional government

It would be absurd to describe government under 'Umar as a despotism, albeit a principled and benevolent one. Rather, it was, beyond any degree that could have been imagined at the time, 'constitutional' in the modern sense. That is, government was according to law, constrained as to its rights and purposes, with the governed made aware of their duty to question the decisions and actions taken either by the head of state or by any of his officials.

Self-evidently, this duty could not be intelligently discharged by the people if the different functions of government were confused. It is a most remarkable achievement of 'Umar's rule that he succeeded, without any precedent in Arab history to follow, in distinguishing the functions of government into separate departments. His reforms were not all carried to completion or perfection (he ruled for only ten years), but they set the pattern for all future governments and administrations under the rule of Islam.

6

Civil Administration

Assimilation of pre-Islamic procedures

The Muslims had no history of imperial government. 'Umar appears to have suffered no inhibitions in principle about either adopting or altering the administrative methods he found in place. He chose whatever way most practicably and effectively served the demands of equity and justice, his responsibilities as a ruler governing in the name of Islam. With regard to such matters as land assessment and taxes, customs duties, auditing, and accounting, he followed the existing laws and usages of Persians and Romans, making only the changes needed to remove injustices and inequities. For example, the rate of *jizya* was not a single fixed rate but varied from place to place. In this, 'Umar followed the practice of Khosrau Anusherwan (Khosrau I), the emperor most admired among the Persians for his justice and wisdom. The Persians therefore found the tax easier to understand and accept.

Administrative divisions and offices

In general, 'Umar retained the provinces and districts in the conquered territories as they had been, making only a few changes. For example, the four major provincial divisions of the Persian empire, namely Iraq, Khurasan, Azerbaijan, and Fars, remained as before, together with their districts. Within Syria, Palestine under the Romans had been a single province comprising ten districts. 'Umar divided it into two provinces with Ayliya as the capital of one and Ramlah the capital of the other. He divided Egypt into two provinces: Upper Egypt (called Sa'id by the Arabs) comprising twenty-eight districts, and Lower Egypt comprising fifteen districts, each with a governing officer under the general governorship of 'Amr b. al-'As. 'Umar created the provinces of Makka, Madina, Syria, Jazira, Basra, and Kufa.

The senior officers in each province were the *Wali* or governor; the *Katib* or chief secretary to the governor; the *Katib al-diwan* or chief secretary of the army secretariat; *Sahib al-kharaj* or collector of revenues; *Sahib bayt al-mal* or treasury officer; and *Qadi* or chief judge. Each province also had a commander-in-chief of the military though, in most cases, the governor exercised this responsibility. As far as is known, the department of police was not separate in every province and the duties of this office were carried out by the *'amils* or collectors of revenue. For example, the *Sahib al-kharaj* of Bahrayn, Qadama b. Maz'un, was also for a time the chief of police there. In Kufa, while 'Ammar b. Yasir was governor, he also served as chief of police; his collector of revenues was 'Uthman b. Hanif; his treasury officer was 'Abdullah b. Mas'ud; his *Qadi* was Shurayh, and his *Katib al-diwan* was 'Abdullah b. Khalaf. The large and permanent staff attached to senior officers at provincial level was appointed directly by the Caliph or with his knowledge and approval. Treasury officers, judges, and others were also appointed to districts under the authority of the provincial governor.

The selection of officers

'Umar's knowledge of the family histories of the Arabs, together with his gift for weighing up the strengths and weaknesses of particular individuals and his understanding of the responsibilities of each appointment, enabled him to choose his officers with exceptional insight. The popular recognition of 'Umar's skill in this regard meant that his appointments, once he had made them (and he consulted before he decided), were respected. Besides 'Umar himself, there were at that time four men who had no equal in the whole of Arabia for statesmanship and administrative competence: Mu'awiya b. Abi Sufyan, 'Amr b. al-'As, Mughira b. Shu'ba, and Ziyad b. Samiyya. Excepting Ziyad, who at sixteen was too young for a senior post, 'Umar appointed these ambitious men to the most senior commands, but they remained entirely loyal and subordinate to the authority of the Caliph. 'Umar was equally alert to talent that was limited in scope: for example, he commended 'Amr b. Ma'di Karab and Tulayha b. Khalid for appointment as military commanders but expressly instructed that neither be given an administrative post.

'Umar moved senior officials around, to test and enlarge their competence in different roles, also to prevent habituation and the consequent danger of abuse. Under his administration, there was no governor save 'Amr b. al-'As (who had rare knowledge of Egypt and its people) who was not moved at least once. He avoided concentration of power in the hands of any individual or individual clan. (Failure to continue this policy after him was a major factor in the civil wars that ensued.) Out of his own clan, Nu'man b. 'Adiy was the only one to be given a senior appointment, and 'Umar removed him from it for a misdemeanour. Men of exceptional influence (that is, potential candidates for the succession) were not permitted long absences from the capital, where their counsel was of more use to the Muslims. When some of them asked leave to go on *jihad*, the Caliph told them they had already rendered sufficient service in that regard, and emphasized the need to maintain unity among them: 'Do not go abroad, lest you scatter to the right and left.' When 'Abd al-Rahman b. 'Awf asked why, 'Umar replied that it was a question best left unanswered (Al-Ya'qubi, 2:158).

No statesman demonstrated better than 'Umar that it is possible to use political skill without resort to cynical or secretive manoeuvring. He invariably gave public notice and public account of his decisions to appoint, transfer, or dismiss state servants. His explanation of the demotion of Khalid and Muthanna, two brilliant commanders, is an example: 'Umar recognized the political (as well as the moral) dangers for the Muslims in the mystique that had accrued around the prowess of these men. Another example, mentioned above, is his refusal to appoint any men of the Hashim clan to provincial governorships.

'Umar's political decisions were based on clear analysis of political realities and foresight in dealing with them. He did not rely upon, and therefore did not inspire against himself, secretive intrigue. He was also wise enough to understand that his officers might be less scrupulous in the discharge of their duties than they should be. He strengthened the ancient Arab custom of 'receiving deputations', making it a regular feature of his administration. Once every year, people came to Madina from all the provinces of the empire to report directly to the Caliph the conditions obtaining in their areas, and to make known to him their needs or grievances. In addition, 'Umar maintained personal agents in every department of state in every district, who reported directly and regularly to him any improper conduct. The dismissal of 'Umar's kinsman, Nu'man, followed information received by this means about his taste for luxurious living. Governors were careful in their policies almost as if 'Umar were able in person to supervise them, and rarely took any serious step without first notifying him.

For his own Chief Secretary, 'Umar chose the esteemed Companion, 'Abdullah b. Arqam. 'Umar was a witness to the occasion when a letter was brought to the Prophet which required a reply. The Prophet asked who would write the reply, and 'Abdullah volunteered for the task and performed it to the Prophet's great satisfaction. 'Umar remembered the man's capability and the Prophet's approval of it, and honoured both by appointing 'Abdullah as his secretary. For some period during 'Umar's caliphate, Zayd b. Thabit also held this important post. Not every appointment was made to please 'Umar's own judgement. For example, somewhat reluctantly, he appointed another Companion, 'Ammar b. Yasir, an elderly Ansari much loved for his holiness and piety but not known for administrative ability or political acumen, to replace

Sa'd b. Abi Waqqas as governor of Kufa. However, as 'Ammar could not govern effectively, 'Umar was soon obliged to depose him, having demonstrated to 'Ammar's partisans that he had not been fit for the post.

The burden of choosing the right men was not, as it could not have been, carried by one man alone, not even by someone as gifted as 'Umar. The Caliph, as noted above, applied to the Assembly to recommend and approve major appointments. At times, some Companions complained that 'Umar was dragging them into worldly entanglements. One such was Abu 'Ubayda. 'Umar had replied that if he could not turn to the Prophet's Companions to help him in affairs of government, to whom could he turn? In his own mind, 'Umar was certain of the need for men who were both competent and pious to participate actively in the responsibilities of administration.

Another difficulty for 'Umar was the reluctance of some of the Companions, Abu 'Ubayda again notable among them, to accept salaries for what they regarded as service to Islam. But a volunteer status for senior officers of state was not compatible with the demands of regular administrative procedures, and 'Umar strove to persuade the Companions to accept salaries and, moreover, in order to prevent future malpractice, fixed the salaries at relatively high levels.

Conditions of appointment

Every man appointed to an office of state was required to promise that he would not ride a Turkish horse or wear fine clothes, nor eat sifted flour, nor keep a porter at his door but, instead, keep his door always open to those who had need of him. These terms were typically included in the document of instruction, stating his power and duties, handed to the man in the presence of Companions, both Muhajirun and Ansar. On taking up office, the man had to have the document read out in public so that the local people also were made aware of its contents. In this way, 'Umar did his best to ensure that the governed knew the limits of the powers of state officials and the rights due to them from those officials. On one occasion, addressing a gathering of officials, 'Umar said to them: 'Remember, I have not appointed you as commanders and tyrants over the people. Rather, I have sent you as leaders so that the people may follow your example. Give the Muslims their rights and do not beat them lest they become abased. Nor praise them unduly lest they fall into the error of conceit. Do not keep your doors shut in their faces lest the more powerful among them eat up the weaker ones. And do not behave as if you were superior to them, for that would be tyranny over them.'

An inventory of the official's wealth and property was made and recorded before he took up appointment. In the event of any unusual improvement in his financial position, he was summoned to explain it and any illegitimate excess confiscated for the public treasury.

All senior officials were required to present themselves in Madina at the time of the annual pilgrimage when Muslims from all over the Islamic world were gathered. In public assembly, the Caliph invited anyone who had a grievance to present it, and pledged himself, if the grievance were upheld, to secure the complainant's right of retaliation or compensation.

Complaints were investigated publicly, sometimes by a committee set up for the purpose, more often by Muhammad b. Maslama, an Ansari Companion. 'Umar chose him for this position because the Prophet had, on the occasion of a military expedition outside Madina, entrusted the city to his care. It is worth noting that 'Umar did not allow political expediency or circumstance to even delay, let alone prevent, inquiry into the conduct of his officials. For example, despite the impending battle of Nihawand against the Persians, he dispatched Muhammad b. Maslama to Kufa to investigate complaints against Sa'd b. Abi Waqqas, the governor there. After Muhammad's investigations, Sa'd was returned to Madina, where the Caliph examined the case further.

Being summoned to Madina was typical of the earlier years of 'Umar's caliphate. It happened in the case of the governor of Basra, Abu Musa Ash'ari. The charges against Abu Musa were that he had reserved sixty well-born prisoners of war for himself, that he owned a female slave who was provided with fine food such as was beyond the means of the average Muslim in Basra, and that he had entrusted the whole business of administration to Ziyad b. Samiyya, who did just as he pleased. On investigation, the first charge was found to be false. To satisfy himself about the third, 'Umar sent for Ziyad and was so content with Abu Musa's delegation of duties to this capable young man that he advised the authorities in Basra to consult him in all affairs. As Abu Musa was unable to offer any adequate response to the second charge, the female slave was accordingly taken away from him.

The Caliph was most severe if he learnt of his officials being haughty or aloof. Those who, for example, omitted to visit the sick or ask after slaves, or to whose courts the poor did not find easy access, were generally dismissed.

Once, while 'Umar was walking in the street in Madina, a man said to him: ' 'Umar! Do you think to escape the punishment of God by devising a few regulations for your officers? Do you not know that 'Iyad b. Ghanam, a governor in Egypt, wears fine clothes and keeps a porter at his door?' (Abu Yusuf, 116). The Caliph at once sent Muhammad b. Maslama to Egypt, ordering him to bring 'Iyad back in whatever state he found him. Muhammad b. Maslama, on arrival in Egypt, found that 'Iyad did indeed have a porter at his door and was wearing a shirt of fine cloth. In the same shirt, 'Iyad was presented to 'Umar. The Caliph ordered him to change it for one of coarse wool, put him in charge of a herd of goats and sent him out to the desert to graze them. 'Iyad protested in vain that death was more agreeable to him than this humiliation. 'Umar retorted that his ('Iyad's) father had been a goatherd and that he should not be ashamed of it. 'Iyad repented sincerely of his faults and performed his duties conscientiously thereafter.

In another and better known case, Sa'd b. Abi Waqqas, the governor of Kufa, had had a palace built, to the front of which an antechamber was attached. 'Umar thought that this might be construed as a device by which the Governor held himself aloof from free access by the people. He therefore ordered Muhammad b. Maslama to burn the antechamber down. The order was carried out while Sa'd looked on.

Such actions do appear to negate the freedom of individuals to conduct their private lives according to their own taste. However, the spirit of equality that 'Umar desired to foster could not have been realized if his most senior officers did not embody it in their own practice. Moreover, the absence of pomp and ceremony was, certainly at that time, a stable feature of the Arabs' character and of their normal relations with each other. It is a fact that the same strictness was not applied by 'Umar to districts where the Arabs were not yet dominant. In Syria, for example, the governor, Mu'awiya b. Abi Sufyan, lived in very high style. 'Umar remarked on this during a visit to the province. Mu'awiya explained that the Romans were habituated to such high manners in their governors and without the prestige associated with this style he could not maintain the authority of the Islamic state. 'Umar accepted this explanation.

PUBLIC REVENUES

The Treasury

During the time of the Prophet, state revenues were no sooner received than distributed, often at a single sitting. Abu Bakr followed the same practice, although during his caliphate a house in Madina was designated as the treasury. On the Caliph's death, accounts showed a balance of only one dirham.

In 15 AH, following the receipt of a large sum of money from Bahrayn, 'Umar convened the Assembly to discuss the question of state revenues and expenditures. A system, like the one in Syria, of a treasury with formal accounting procedures to regulate expenditures such as the maintenance of the army was proposed and approved. He established a central treasury in the capital, Madina, and appointed 'Abdullah b. Arqam to manage it. Treasuries were subsequently set up also in provincial capitals with their own chief officers under the supervision of provincial governors.

To house the treasuries, 'Umar ordered the construction of strong and grand buildings, although for other public buildings he usually demanded every possible economy. In Kufa, Ruzbih, a famous Magian architect, built a treasury using materials from former imperial palaces. When this building was broken into and robbed, 'Umar instructed Sa'd b. Abi Waqqas to have it joined on to the mosque which, being always full of people, would ensure the security of the treasury. This measure was carried out and sufficed, during the caliphate of 'Umar, to remove fear of theft. In later times, however, armed guards were necessary to secure treasury buildings. One historian records that, when Talha and Zubayr rose in rebellion against 'Ali, they went to Basra to seize the treasury but were resisted by a guard of forty soldiers.

Provincial treasuries held funds sufficient to meet their routine expenditures, the balance being remitted to Madina at the end of each year. Accounts were kept on long sheets rolled up for storage. The accounts were necessarily very detailed—for example, even distinguishing features, colours, and ages of livestock received in *zakah* payments were recorded—and 'Umar insisted on their accuracy, sometimes making the entries himself. It is no small tribute to 'Umar's influence and authority that the Arabs were able, in a relatively short time, to learn how to keep written accounts of revenues and expenditures. Not all were willing to do so. One of the reasons for the dismissal of Khalid was his refusal to submit, for 'Umar's inspection, detailed accounts of military expenditures and gains from spoils of war.

For the Treasury to follow revenues and expenditures closely, it had to be provided with detailed land records and (for *zakah* and *jizya* levies) population counts. To a large extent, the existing methods for keeping land records and censuses were retained with only minor amendments. Also (see below), they were maintained in the languages and, mostly, by the same people as before. It would have been quite impossible, given the very few Muslims competent to do so during 'Umar's caliphate, to run and maintain such records in Arabic.

Lands subject to kharaj

Before Islam, various Arab dynasties had established small kingdoms in the Peninsula but had never organized a land revenue system. In the early days of Islam, after the conquest of Khaybar, the Jews there had asked the Prophet to leave the conquered lands in their possession and, in lieu of taxes, to accept half of the produce of those lands. Since the Jews were well acquainted with agriculture and the Muslims were not, the Prophet had acquiesced. Where the inhabitants of conquered lands embraced Islam, tithes had been levied as a form of *zakah*. Later on, during the rule of Abu Bakr, when parts of Arab Iraq were conquered, no form of regular land tax was settled, a lump sum payment being agreed instead.

Thus, 'Umar had no sufficient precedent in Muslim history or experience on which to base a coherent land revenue system. However, following the great battles of Yarmuk and Qadisiya that, respectively, secured the territories of Syria and Arab Iraq for the Muslims, he set his mind to this task.

The first major hurdle he faced was the insistence of army commanders and other senior Muslims (among them no less a figure than 'Abd al-Rahman b. 'Awf) that conquered territories and their inhabitants should be distributed among the conquerors. On 'Umar's instruction, Sa'd b. Abi Waqqas had taken a census of the areas of Iraq then under Muslim control. From this census, it was calculated that three persons would fall to the lot of each Muslim soldier. 'Umar argued that, if lands and people were distributed in this way, the state and future generations of Muslims would be deprived of sources of revenue for, among other purposes, defence and the maintenance of law and order. This argument was resisted in public debate over several days by those who supported the rights of the conquerors. All the Muhajirun were present at this debate and five representatives from each of the two major tribal divisions of the Ansar. 'Umar received the backing of some senior figures such as 'Ali, 'Uthman and Talha, but as many more eminent Companions resisted persuasion. Finally, in a forceful speech, 'Umar recited, from sura *al-Hashr*, the Qur'anic verses (59.7–10) that indicate that spoils of war should be reserved for refugees, the homeless, the poor and needy, and for 'those who come after them', that is, for the Muslims of the future. In the end, 'Umar's argument was endorsed unanimously and this principle firmly established: conquered lands were at the disposal of the state, that is, of the Muslims as a whole, and the former occupants would not be dispossessed.

The land settlement of Iraq

'Umar first apprised himself fully of how the existing system operated, aiming to improve rather than to replace it. Under the Persians, all cultivable land had been assessed at a certain rate, recovered in three instalments. Under Khosrau Anusherwan, the rate had not been allowed to exceed half the land's produce, but later emperors had been considerably more demanding. 'Umar began by ordering a new and comprehensive survey of the conquered lands in Iraq. He entrusted the task to two eminent Companions, 'Uthman b. Hanif and Hudhayfa b. al-Yaman, both with experience in this work gained from long years of residence in Iraq: 'Uthman was particularly proficient and earned a reputation for measuring land as precisely as cloth is measured. Their work was done with great care and took several months, the measure used being prepared and verified by the Caliph himself.

The country was measured at 375 miles long by 240 miles wide with a cultivable land area, excluding mountains and deserts, of 36 million *jaribs*. Out of this total, lands that had formerly been the property of the imperial estate, endowments of fire-temples, the lands of those who had died without heirs or fled the country, the lands of rebels, lands set aside to meet the expense of building and maintaining roads and for the expense of the post, and 'new' lands recovered from rivers and forests, were declared the property of the Islamic state. The income from these lands was reserved for works of public utility. It is also from these lands that estates were granted to reward exceptional service to Islam, although such estates remained taxable in the same way as other private holdings. The remaining lands were left in the possession of their former occupants and assessed for tax. The rate varied according to the crop grown, for example six dirhams per *jarib* for sugar-cane, two dirhams per *jarib* for wheat, and one for barley. The rate also varied to take account of soil fertility: thus, on the better quality lands the rates for wheat and barley were, respectively, four and two dirhams per *jarib*.

The total revenue for the lands assessed in Iraq came in the first year to 86 million dirhams, a sum that amounted, overall, to rather less than half the total value of the land's produce. This made the assessment more favourable to landowners and cultivators than in the time of Khosrau I. Furthermore, the great Persian landlords of pre-Islamic days were allowed to retain most of their ancient rights and privileges. It is therefore unsurprising that, even though some individual rates were higher than in the time of Khosrau I, produce increased dramatically and fresh lands were brought into cultivation. Revenue increased to over 100 million dirhams in the second year and continued to increase thereafter. 'Umar was scrupulously careful to check that neither Muslims nor *dhimmis* (non-Muslim subjects) had been put to any hardship in the collection of these taxes. When revenues were brought to the capital, 'Umar sent for ten reliable and upright men from both Basra and Kufa and questioned them on oath about the condition of the people, especially the *dhimmis*. In the reigns of subsequent caliphs, the rates of assessment were increased considerably but the total revenues then obtained never equalled those obtained in the time of 'Umar.

Egypt

'Umar did not set up for any other country a land settlement such as the one he ordered for Iraq. He retained the existing system and the existing records, and the Persians or Greeks or Copts employed in the land revenue department of the previous administration continued to work in their posts and to keep books in the language they had used previously. However, the Caliph did address and try to remove such shortcomings and injustices in the system as were brought to his notice.

In Egypt, the Romans had kept the land revenue system inherited from the Ptolemies, which they in turn had inherited and maintained, with little amendment, from the Pharaohs. The whole land had been measured and the tax on it was assessed and collected according to three rules: taxes could be paid in cash or kind; the land was assessed on average yield over the years of each settlement; the settlement was revised every four years. The Romans had added the further demands that a large quantity of grain should be shipped annually to Constantinople, and another large quantity set aside to supply the Roman garrisons. The first reform 'Umar effected was to abolish these extra levies outright. It is certainly true that grain was imported to the Arab Peninsula from Egypt during times of famine, but these imports were taken as part or in lieu of the land tax and were not an additional burden. In later periods, for example during the caliphate of Mu'awiya, when the tax was paid in cash, the grain imported from Egypt was bought in cash, and records of these transactions are known. Similarly, grain for the stores that 'Umar had set aside in each province for the use of the army were likewise taken in lieu of taxes due and were not an additional charge.

'Umar also reformed the collection system, making it easier for the cultivators. As agricultural yield was dependent in Egypt on the variable Nile floods, an assessment on the average produce over a number of years was both uncertain and unfair on cultivators who could not necessarily husband their resources against lean years. In the new system introduced by 'Umar, landlords, owners of large estates, and expert assessors were called upon, when the time of assessment approached, to estimate the expected yield and the taxes due on it for the country as a whole. Then, after consultation with local cultivators and collectors, estimates were prepared for each district and sub-district, village by village. Revenues assigned to churches, public baths, and Muslim guest houses were the first charge on the produce, and taxes were then calculated on what remained after these deductions. Village artisans also had to pay a share of the taxes assessed on their village, the average rate being one dinar per *jarib*. The system was certainly tedious and cumbersome, requiring a fresh settlement each year, but it was perceived to be, and was, fairer than the one it replaced.

The reward for the moderation and equity 'Umar achieved in the system was that the revenues from the lands of Egypt were far greater than in subsequent periods—12 million dinars as against 3 million under the later Umayyads and 'Abbasids. When 'Abdullah b. Sa'd, the governor of Egypt during the caliphate of 'Uthman, collected 14 million, 'Uthman remarked that the she-camel had yielded more milk that year. On hearing that, 'Amr b. al-'As commented bitterly: 'Yes, but its young had starved.' The caliphate of Mu'awiya was generally a period of prosperity and progress for the Muslims, but the average land revenues from Egypt had by then already fallen to 9 million dinars.

Syria and elsewhere

In Syria, the existing land revenue system was adopted unchanged. The lands were already classed according to their quality and degree of fertility and assessed on that basis. The average of revenues collected in Syria during 'Umar's caliphate amounted to 14 million dinars.

The sources do not give much information about either the administration or assessment of land taxes in the conquered territories of the Persian heartlands and beyond. They mention the fact that *jizya* was imposed, and the amount thereof, and that lands were assessed as to revenue and, in some cases, lump sum payments agreed.

The rationale of 'Umar's reforms

'Umar aimed to remove the glaring injustices in the existing land revenue system and to encourage and improve agriculture. His reforms undoubtedly succeeded in both aims.

The Romans, when they conquered Syria and Egypt, dispossessed the native population. All arable lands were seized; most were divided up among army commanders and court officials, with a part reserved as imperial estates and a part assigned to the Church. The former owners became little more than tied labourers or serfs, without right of property in the lands they worked, and were transferred with ownership of the land. Later, towards the time of the Muslim conquest, the native people had begun to acquire rights of property in land, but the exercise of their rights was at the mercy of Roman overlords. This usage was not restricted to the Roman empire but prevailed generally at that time.

Most of the Roman landlords fled the territories with the Roman garrisons defeated and expelled by the Muslims. Those who remained were deprived of their unlawful holdings. Imperial estates and other lands formerly owned by Roman commanders were returned to the natives of the country. The Muslims, as noted above, were not granted possession of the conquered lands, indeed they were forbidden even to purchase land. This rule remained in force for at least fifty years after the caliphate of 'Umar, a fact that may be deduced from the allusions to it as a legal precedent in the writings of, among others, Imam Malik. 'Umar went further and also forbade the Arabs who migrated to the new territories from engaging in agriculture. He expressly wrote to all provincial governors that, as the Muslims were given state stipends, they should have no need to seek an income from agriculture. The Caliph no doubt sought, by this measure, to preserve their martial valour and their commitment to the army.

The assessment of land for taxes was, as we saw, arranged to provide revenue for the state without overburdening those who managed or worked the land. There is no question that the equity and moderation of the system during 'Umar's rule greatly facilitated the extension of the Muslim conquests and the spread of Islam. It is also relevant to note that 'Umar made a point of inviting the opinion of the non-Muslims when their lands were assessed and attended fully to their suggestions and objections. For example, in connection with the revenue settlement in Egypt, 'Umar instructed his governors to consult the local people and himself sent for a Copt well versed in the subject of land taxation and discussed it with him in Madina.

'Umar was as much concerned that agriculture should be improved and extended as with the problem of deriving revenues from it equitably. He had it proclaimed that anyone who brought new land into cultivation would be granted rights of ownership over it. On the other hand, anyone who took possession of land but failed to cultivate it within three years would lose rights of ownership. As a result of this measure, very extensive areas of land were made productive for the first time. Those people who had fled their homes and lands at the time of invasion were invited by public proclamation to return and resume possession and use of their lands.

Irrigation works such as building of dams, channels, and sluices to facilitate the distribution of water were funded from the public treasury. One historian records that, in Egypt alone, 120,000 labourers were employed for a whole year in such projects and paid out of the public treasury. With 'Umar's permission, Juza' b. Mu'awiya constructed several canals in the districts of Khuzistan and Ahwaz, which enabled large areas of land to be brought under cultivation for the first time. Scores of similar examples are detailed in the sources.

Lands subject to 'ushr

Lands held by Muslims were not subject to *kharaj* but to a different tax, the rate of which had been fixed by the Prophet at one-tenth of the produce or *'ushr*, and which was counted as a part of *zakah*. These *'ushri* lands were either (a) Arab lands whose owners had embraced Islam in earlier days; (b) lands formerly owned by a non-Muslim subject which had passed into the possession of a Muslim by the former's death without issue, or flight from the country, or revolt, or formal abandonment of them; or (c) lands not previously owned by anyone but brought under cultivation by a Muslim. During the reign of 'Umar, lands in the conquered territories which came into Muslim ownership and which were irrigated by canals or wells built by the previous, non-Muslim, owners were subject to *kharaj*; if, however, the irrigation was added by the Muslim owners, the lands were subject to *'ushr.*

The difference between *'ushr* and *kharaj* was not, as it appears, an unjust discrimination in favour of Muslim landowners. First, Muslims had to pay more items of tax than *dhimmis* (non-Muslims)—the latter were exempt from the *zakah* charged on live-stock, horses, and cash which Muslims were obliged to pay. In any case, the Muslims owned very little land in comparison with non-Muslims. Second, *'ushr* could never be reduced or remitted, even if the Caliph desired it, whereas *kharaj* could be reduced or remitted, as sometimes happened. Third, *kharaj* was charged only once in a year, whereas *'ushr* was paid on each crop through-out the year.

Other sources of revenue

Besides *kharaj* and *'ushr*, the other sources of public funds were *zakah*, *'ushur*, *jizya*, and one-fifth of the spoils of war.

The law and rules of *zakah* were fully formulated during the time of the Prophet. This tax was levied uniquely on Muslims and no part of a Muslim's property or income, including livestock, was exempt from it. The only change 'Umar instituted was the imposition of *zakah* on horses not used for riding but traded as merchandise. (In the Prophet's time, horses had not been traded in this way and he had exempted them on that basis.)

'Ushur were an innovation of 'Umar's in response to a report from Abu Musa Ash'ari that Muslim traders were being charged a 10 per cent import duty on their merchandise when they entered foreign lands. 'Umar imposed the same charge on merchants from those countries when their goods first entered Muslim lands. Eventually, the rule was extended to all the conquered territories and a customs department was established that collected a con-siderable revenue. The rates charged were fixed at 10 per cent (*'ushur*) for foreigners, 5 per cent for *dhimmis* (non-Muslim sub-jects), and 2.5 per cent for Muslims. Duties were imposed on articles

above a value of 200 dirhams openly carried for the purpose of trade—officials were specifically instructed not to search personal luggage. The charge was levied once only at the point of entry, the merchants being free to move their goods thereafter anywhere within Muslim territories for a year.

Jizya was a tax levied on non-Muslims who entered into peace treaty with the Muslims. It was, from the first, a charge in lieu of military service or in return for defence by the Muslims of the non-Muslims' persons and properties. As noted in the narrative of the conquests, when the Muslim forces were obliged to withdraw from the western districts of Syria, the jizya payments collected from the inhabitants of Hims, Damascus, and other cities were returned to them in full. Equally, when military service was accepted from any non-Muslims they were exempted from jizya, or payments already taken were returned. 'Umar himself wrote to the military commanders in Iraq urging them: 'Take such military service as you need from mounted soldiers and exempt them from jizya.' In 22 AH, when Azerbaijan was conquered, its people were given this written assurance: 'Those who serve in the [Muslim] army in any one year will be exempt from jizya for that year.' Similar terms were agreed for Armenia and Jurjan in the same year. It is important, too, that revenues from jizya were disbursed exclusively for provisions, clothes, and other necessities of the army. In the early years, a part of the jizya was collected in kind. In Egypt, for example, the assessment per head was four dirhams, of which two were collected in cash and two in equivalent values of wheat, olive oil, honey, and vinegar. Later on, when a separate army commissariat had been established, jizya was collected in cash only.

THE ADMINISTRATION OF JUSTICE

During the brief caliphate of Abu Bakr, the Caliph himself and his governors also acted as judges. During the longer rule of 'Umar, administration was developed much further and 'Umar was able to separate the judiciary from other departments of state, establish courts of justice, and appoint qadis. He also elaborated the fundamentals of judicial procedure summarized in this famous instruction addressed to judges:

Praise be to God. Justice is the [most] important obligation [of your office]. Treat the people equally in your presence, in your company, and in your decisions, so that the weak do not despair of justice and those in high positions have no hope of your favour. The burden of proof lies with the plaintiff, and he who denies must do so on oath. Compromise is permissible so long as it does not make the unlawful lawful or the lawful unlawful. Let nothing prevent you from revising your decision of yesterday after due consideration [persuades you that your former decision was incorrect]. When, in doubt on a question, you find nothing relevant in the Qur'an or Sunna of the Prophet, think over the question again, then again. Ponder over the precedents and analogous cases, then decide by analogy. A term should be fixed for one who wishes to produce witnesses: if he then establishes his case, grant him his right; otherwise, his suit should be dismissed. All Muslims are trustworthy [as witnesses] except those who have been punished with flogging or who [are known to] have borne false witness, or who are doubtful in inheritance and relationship. (Shirazi, 39–40; Mawardi, 119–20)

The Law

As the source of law in Islam is the Qur'an, not the head of state, nor the people or their representatives, there was no formal legislating activity. However, for matters on which the Qur'an is silent or does not provide the necessary details, recourse is allowed to the practice and precepts (the Sunna) of the Prophet, then to the *ijma'* or consensus of informed Muslim opinion, and then to *qiyas* or reasoned analogy. In an instruction to Qadi Shurayh, the chief judge in Kufa, 'Umar explained this procedure for reaching verdicts, adding that, if it did not suffice for the case in hand, the judge must decide by his own reasoning.

'Umar also recorded and dispatched to provincial and district judges his own verdicts or fatwas on a number of particularly difficult and weighty questions. These judgements are extant in various sources and would, if collected, make up a short code of laws.

Examples of these and their rationale are discussed separately in Chapter 8.

Appointment of judges

'Umar's care and insight in the selection of judges may be gauged from the quality of men he appointed. In Madina itself he appointed Zayd b. Thabit. Zayd had been the Prophet's amanuensis responsible for recording the revelations of the Qur'an. Besides Arabic, he was also proficient in Syriac and Hebrew, and he was universally acclaimed by the Muslims as the supreme authority in the Law concerned with obligations. In Palestine, 'Umar appointed 'Ubada b. al-Samit, one of the Companions who had memorized the Qur'an in the lifetime of the Prophet. The Prophet had chosen him to instruct the *ashab al-suffa*, those impoverished Muslims who spent their days and nights in the Mosque in total dedication to Islam. In Kufa, 'Umar appointed 'Abdullah b. Mas'ud, a man of unquestioned scholarship and judicial acumen and generally regarded as the first founder of what became the Hanafi Law. In 19 AH, 'Abdullah was succeeded as Qadi by Shurayh, not a Companion, but widely esteemed for his penetrating intelligence and wisdom, and to this day mentioned as a model for all judges. 'Ali called him the greatest judge among the Arabs.

'Umar forbade judges to engage in trade or to buy and sell in the market-place. With the same motive of preventing corruption, he fixed relatively high salaries. 'Umar also established the rule that only those who were both financially and socially well placed should be considered for appointment as judges: a wealthy man would be less tempted to take bribes; a man of high position was less likely to be influenced by the social rank of a plaintiff or defendant.

For justice to be effective, it needs to be accessible as well as fair. Judges were therefore appointed in sufficient numbers, one to each administrative district, to serve the Muslims there—the non-Muslims had their own separate provisions to deal with disputes among themselves. No special expenses were involved in bringing suits, and mosques were used as court-houses—no other public buildings were (or could be) better designed or sited for ease and freedom of access to the public. Judges were expressly instructed to treat poor litigants with gentleness and courtesy so that they did not feel intimidated and could put their case without fear.

Jurisconsults

The institution of legal consultation (*ifta'*), unique to Islam, existed from the time of the Prophet and had continued under Abu Bakr. 'Umar extended it and made it more reliable and effective. He appointed learned and capable men to every large centre of popu- lation with the task of responding to public queries about the law so that no one should have cause to plead ignorance of it or uncertainty. 'Umar was fully aware of the dangerous conse- quences of irresponsible or ill-informed individuals pronouncing upon the Law. He therefore allowed authority to interpret the Law only to men he had personally questioned, approved, and appointed. Among the most famous of these were 'Ali, 'Uthman, Mu'adh b. Jabal, 'Abd al-Rahman b. 'Awf, Ubayy b. Ka'b, Zayd b. Thabit, Abu Hurayra and Abu Darda'. The people were notified of the names of such authorized jurisconsults, and their fields of special expertise or excellence, by announcement in the mosques. When necessary, 'Umar re-examined particular individuals to ensure that their legal opinions and reasoning were sound. This happened several times in the case of no less a figure than Abu Hurayra. Also, 'Umar forbade any man to pronounce on the Law who did not have the Caliph's permission to do so. 'Abdullah b. Mas'ud, Qadi of Kufa, was once censured in this respect. 'Umar's strict care and vigilant supervision of this institution were not, unfor- tunately, maintained after him.

PUBLIC WELFARE

'Umar's anxious concern for the welfare of his subjects flowed directly from the reiterated injunctions of the Qur'an to look after the needs of the poor, orphans, widows, and captives (that is, slaves). Some of the most enduring and most rehearsed images of 'Umar as the ideal Muslim ruler relate to his efforts to put the Qur'anic injunctions into effect.

'Umar interpreted the Qur'anic phrase 'the poor and the needy' to refer respectively to the Muslims and the People of the Book. Officers who distributed funds from the public treasury for poor relief were instructed and acted accordingly. Foundlings (abandoned children) were nursed and brought up at the state's expense: maintenance began at 100 dirhams a year and increased by small increments annually as the child grew up. Orphans without means were similarly looked after; those who owned some property had it managed as a trust while they were minors. When 'Umar noted that the value of properties entrusted to him on behalf of some orphans was being depleted by the obligatory *zakah* charge, he ordered Hakam b. Abi al-'As to trade with the orphans' wealth and pay the profits into their estates. Travellers were served with food at public guest houses at the state's expense. 'Umar often went in person to see the travellers properly looked after in the guest house in Madina.

Great suffering and hardships came to the people of Arabia in the year of famine, 18 AH. 'Umar tackled the crisis with wonderful energy. When cash and food stores held in Madina were exhausted, he ordered the commanders in Iraq and Syria to send grain in whatever quantities they could. Abu 'Ubayda dispatched 4,000 camel-loads of grain from Syria. 'Amr b. al-'As procured some 5,000 tons of grain in Egypt and from the Red Sea shipped them to Jar, about three days from Madina. 'Umar himself attended the arrival of one of the ships whose precious cargo was unloaded into two buildings specially constructed for the purpose. A register of people in most need was written by Zayd b. Thabit and coupons bearing the seal of 'Umar were issued against the names on it. The grain was then distributed in exchange for the coupons.

While the famine lasted, 'Umar restricted his own diet to barley bread; he refused oil, meat, and other foodstuffs. He used to pray: 'O God, do not destroy the people of [the Prophet] Muhammad for my sins!' His slave Aslam reports that if the famine had lasted much longer than it did, the Caliph would have died from sheer anxiety (Ibn Sa'd, 3:315, 320).

As noted above, 'Umar received annual deputations from all over the empire, from whom he inquired about the conditions of the people. On his tour of Syria, 'Umar travelled without guard or retinue and therefore generally went unrecognized. He was thus able to learn at first hand what people thought of his government. He made arrangements for the widows and orphans who had lost their breadwinners because of the wars or the plague. He had planned similar tours elsewhere in the conquered territories but was assassinated before he could carry out his plans.

In Madina, it was his regular custom to stay on in the Mosque after the congregational prayers and wait for anyone in need who might wish to see him. At night, he often walked within and around the city boundaries, and made inquiries if he saw something amiss. His slave Aslam reports that one night he went to Sarar, about three miles out of Madina, where he saw a woman apparently cooking something with her children crying around her. He asked what the matter was and learnt that the woman, having nothing to cook, was merely going through the motions in order to distract the children. The Caliph returned to the city, took some dates, flour, meat, and oil from the Treasury stores and asked Aslam to load them on his back. Aslam offered to carry them, but 'Umar insisted on doing so himself, just as, on the Day of Judgement, no one else could relieve him of his burdens. He returned to the woman with the supplies and tended the fire while she cooked. He was greatly consoled to see the children happy again. The woman in thanking him said he was better fitted to be Caliph than 'Umar.

There are many anecdotes of this kind. It is possible that the affectionate memory of those telling them has embroidered or added particular details. What is certain is that, even when preoccupied by great affairs of state, 'Umar did not forget the welfare of his subjects individually. Therefore, after the end of the day's business, he would exert himself to find out about and, if he could, supply their needs.

7

Military Administration

Register of men in service

During the rule of Abu Bakr, spoils of war were divided among those who had served in the campaign, ten dirhams for each man in the first year and twenty in the second. Otherwise, there was no military organization, no register of men in service, no fixed salaries, no war office. This situation continued in the first years of 'Umar's caliphate. However, by 15 AH, an army register and a war department had clearly formed. The register was called the *Diwan*, the Persian origin of the word suggesting the origin of the model 'Umar had in mind for adaptation.

'Umar began by commissioning a list of all the tribes of Quraysh and all the tribes of the Madinans or Ansar. The list began with the near kin of the Prophet and continued down the further lines of descent. In this way, 'Umar (of the first four caliphs, the furthest removed in kinship from the Prophet) ensured that his own name came quite a way down a list that was, necessarily, viewed as a roll of honour. The register also made note of dependants in the households of the men listed.

To begin with, the register included all Muslims eligible for state stipends. By 21 AH it served explicitly as a list of those available for military service, actively or as reserves. Annual salaries were initially as follows: for those Muslims who had participated in the battle of Badr, 5,000 dirhams; for those who had suffered the trials of the first emigration to Abyssinia, 4,000 dirhams; the same sum for those who had taken part in the battle of Uhud; for those who had migrated to Madina before the conquest of Makka, 3,000 dirhams; for those who embraced Islam after the conquest of Makka, 2,000; for those who had fought in the battles of Qadisiya and Yarmuk, 300, and for the rest without distinction, 200 dirhams. Salaries were also fixed for the wives and children of the men listed, and graduated proportionately. Slaves listed under any category received exactly the same salaries as free men in the same category, even if the latter were their masters.

Military headquarters

'Umar set up eight major military centres or headquarters, namely at Madina, Kufa, Basra, Fustat, Mosul, Hims, Damascus, Jerusalem, and one in Jordan. Kufa and Basra served as the bases for military operations into Persia and Khuzistan and other eastward campaigns; Fustat was the main centre for reserves needed to defend Egypt and Mosul for the province of Jazira. The number of centres allocated to Syria indicates the size and importance of this province, and its vulnerability to attacks by the Roman fleet as well as from the Roman strongholds in the contiguous region of Asia Minor.

In each centre, large barracks were constructed to house the troops. Other buildings held army stores and provisions, and all the records pertaining to men and equipments. Also, stables were maintained, capable of servicing 4,000 horses for the army's use, with lands at a reasonable distance for pasturing the horses. These stables provided in all a reserve cavalry of 32,000, equipped to move at short notice. 'Umar himself took charge of the cavalry reserve held in Madina.

Military cantonments

'Umar settled some troops in the major towns and cities in the conquered territories, and very substantial garrisons at other strategic points such as borders. In this way, Muslim troops, predominantly but not exclusively Arabs, and their families, were spread throughout the empire.

During his tour of Syria, 'Umar visited all the border towns and inspected the defence arrangements, in particular of the coastal cities and fortresses that were vulnerable to the Roman navy. When Mu'awiya b. Abi Sufyan became governor of the province, he urged the Caliph to do yet more. 'Umar ordered the necessary repairs and reinforcements, additional observation points, and arrangements for the lighting of fires to warn of enemy approach. The Muslims had no fleet at this time to oppose the Romans at sea.

In Egypt, the main military force was concentrated, as noted above, at Fustat, under the command of 'Amr b. al-'As. Following an attempt by the Romans to recapture Alexandria by sea, 'Umar ordered that a quarter of the whole Muslim force in Egypt should be permanently dispatched to the defence of Alexandria, another quarter to the defence of other coastal cities, while the remaining half should stay, under 'Amr's command, at Fustat.

There was very little danger of internal revolt in either Syria or Egypt. The local Christian populations by overwhelming majority preferred Muslim rule to that of the Romans. There was some threat from the Roman power in Asia Minor but the land forces of the Muslims were sufficient in numbers and morale to cope. In the former Persian dominions, the situation was different. Basra and Kufa, both safely near Arabia proper, were beyond doubt secure. Kufa had the largest number of permanently stationed troops, as many as 40,000 on active duty, with a quarter of these always away on front-line service. Spreading outwards from these two headquarters, 'Umar garrisoned all the former Persian cantonments, repairing and extending them where needed, all the way to Khuzistan, Rayy, Azerbaijan, and beyond. Some of the garrisons were very substantial: in Azerbaijan, for example, there were at one time 10,000 regularly stationed troops.

Recruitment

The army register began with the Muhajirun and the Ansar and expanded steadily to include the Arab tribes across the whole

Peninsula and Bahrayn, and then the Arabs who settled in the conquered territories. Enlistment in the army was not restricted to Arabs, however, nor even to Muslims. For example, the elite imperial guard of the Persian emperor, not themselves native Persians, who took part in many of the actions against the Muslim forces at Qadisiya, deserted the Persians during the battle and embraced Islam. Sa'd b. Abi Waqqas settled them in Kufa and put them on the army payroll, and their part in subsequent Islamic conquests is recorded by historians. Another elite corps, in this case well-trained and armoured Persian knights, surrendered at the fall of Sus (20 AH) on condition that they might fight alongside the Muslims and not pay the *jizya*. Abu Musa Ash'ari, who received their surrender, agreed the terms after receiving the Caliph's permission to do so. Later, these knights were settled at Basra and put on the payroll. Also after the battle of Sus, Jats from the Sind region of India, formerly serving the Persians, came over to the Muslim side; they later embraced Islam and were settled at Basra. Romans and Greeks who fought alongside the Arabs in the campaign in Egypt, some 500 in number, were settled by 'Amr b. al-'As in separate districts in Fustat. Also during this campaign, it is recorded that 1,000 Jews fought under the Muslim banner, and those among them who embraced Islam were likewise settled at Fustat.

Pay and provisions

'Umar was anxious that the men who served in the army should be independent of any need to engage, for their livelihoods, in trade, agriculture, or any other occupation that might diminish their commitment or their valour. Salaries were therefore generous and at one point 'Umar increased them. The lowest rate of pay was raised from 200 to 300 dirhams a year; the rate for officers from 7,000 to 10,000; stipends for children normally payable from when they were weaned were paid from the date of their birth. Every tribal unit in the army had its leader or *'arif* and salaries were disbursed to individual soldiers and officers through these leaders. Promotions to a higher rate of pay were made on the basis of length of service or to reward exceptionally distinguished action.

In addition to fixed salaries, spoils of war were distributed among those who had taken part in the action, according to rank. On occasion, the sums involved could be considerable: it is recorded, for example, that cavalrymen engaged in some of the action at Jalula received 9,000 dirhams each, and at Nihawand 6,000 each.

There was little organized provisioning of the armed forces in the early years of 'Umar's rule, not even when they were on active campaign. For example, on the Qadisiya expedition, only meat rations were supplied from Madina. Otherwise, the troops depended for provisions on raiding and plundering the stores of the enemy. After the major conquests, army needs could be and were more regularly supplied through receipt of *jizya* payments in kind rather than cash. In Egypt and Jazira, grains, olive oil, honey, and vinegar were collected for the army. As this method was both cumbersome and inefficient, and the people complained about it, the Caliph commuted all *jizya* payments into cash. A formal commissariat was then set up responsible for the purchase and distribution of provisions for the army. In Syria, 'Amr b. 'Utba was appointed head of this department of army business called *ahra'*, a word (like the department) of Greek origin. Supplies were gathered in one place and distributed monthly: according to the sources (in equivalent measures), 104 lb of grain and 24 lb each of olive oil and vinegar per head. Horses were provided and maintained by the soldiers who used them, not by the state; exceptionally, for needy individuals on the lowest rate of pay, horses were provided from the stock held, under 'Umar's direct supervision, at Madina.

Operations

It was an innovation of 'Umar that every military expedition was accompanied by, besides surgeons and physicians, an officer of the Treasury or accountant, a *qadi*, and interpreters. Every significant army unit was also accompanied by secret reporters who regularly sent written dispatches to the Caliph, detailing the activities of that unit, the state of morale, and any breaches of discipline. By this means 'Umar was able to supervise effectively a large army spread far and wide from the capital, and either prevent or promptly correct any misconduct.

To improve the Arabs' native fighting skills, 'Umar urged army officers to train soldiers in swimming, riding, archery, and marching barefoot. There is no indication in the sources that any kind of parade drills or marches were practised. Before Islam came to the Arabs, their manner of doing battle was this: the opposing hosts would face each other and, after some rounds of single combat between champions, a general action ensued. Division of the fighters into sections, and fighting in organized ranks, were introduced during the time of the Prophet. Even so, each section was separately commanded and moved on the field according to the best judgement and initiative of its leader. The idea of an overall battle plan under a single, unified command was not fully in evidence until Yarmuk, and is attributed to the great Khalid.

The different sections of the army as recognized in the science of war at this time were: *qalb* or command centre; *muqaddama* or vanguard; *maymana* and *maysara*, right and left wings respectively; *saqa* or rearguard and behind it the *rid'* or extreme rear; then, the *talay'a* or scouting patrols, and *ra'id* or foraging parties. Besides the infantry (*rajil*), the separate units were: the camel corps (*rukban*), the cavalry (*farsan*) and the archers (*ramat*).

Espionage was extremely well organized and effective. Spies were recruited from among those Arabs of Iraq and Syria who had embraced Islam but not yet disclosed the fact. They mingled easily with the Christians or Magians among whom they lived and could obtain information about enemy positions and intentions more or less at will. Such intelligence made a significant contribution to the victories at Qadisiya, Yarmuk, and Tikrit. The non-Muslim inhabitants of Damascus and other captured cities from which the Muslims withdrew favoured their recapture and, without expectation of reward, assisted the Muslims by providing invaluable information. The Samaritans, a Jewish sect resident in the Palestine and Jordan area, were specially commissioned to do espionage work, which they carried out in exchange for remission of land taxes.

Catapults were first used by the Muslims in the siege of Ta'if in 8 AH. Their extensive use during the reign of 'Umar was supplemented by the *dabbaba*, a many-tiered wooden tower on wheels, manned by stone-throwers, archers, and wall-piercers, and pushed up to the walls of the fortification. Clearance and construction of roads and bridges and similar works were generally carried out for the Muslim armies by the conquered peoples. In Egypt, where operations around the Nile delta made such works particularly important, a specific agreement to this effect was made with the local Copts—an indication of the hatred they felt for their Roman overlords, and of their hopes of better treatment at the hands of the Muslims.

8

Islam and Islamic Law

The Caliph as Imam

'Umar's highest responsibility, as the Muslims' leader, was the protection and propagation of Islam. 'Islam' is the proper name for a civilization rather than a religious cult, but one whose core is nevertheless the guidance of the Qur'an and Sunna. Seen from a Muslim perspective, 'Umar's successes on the field of battle and in administrative reform are called successes because they flowed from and contributed to his highest achievement, namely, promoting the wider understanding of Qur'an and Sunna. Achievement in this respect was necessarily general and diffuse, impossible to measure precisely in the way that increase in revenues or territory can be measured. Nevertheless, 'Umar did explicitly concern himself with the protection and propagation of Islam. His actions in this regard were sufficiently consistent and coherent to be called policies. We shall now give a brief account of these policies—the preservation and teaching of the Qur'an and Sunna; the evolution of the Law derived therefrom; and the prevention of misguidance.

The Qur'an

The Qur'an was not collected in written form in one single place during the Prophet's lifetime. Rather, portions of it were written out on diverse materials in the safe-keeping of different Companions. However, a considerable number of Companions had the whole Qur'an stored in their memories. When, during the apostasy wars, many of them were slain, 'Umar urged the Caliph, Abu Bakr, to collect the whole Qur'an in written form. Abu Bakr said he could not do what the Prophet himself had omitted to do. But 'Umar pressed his argument until the Caliph was persuaded. Zayd b. Thabit (the Prophet's amanuensis) was commissioned to oversee the work. A public proclamation required whoever kept any portion of the Qur'an learnt directly from the Prophet to bring it forward, and to produce two witnesses who would confirm that they had seen the particular verses in written form during the Prophet's lifetime. When all the verses had been collected, Zayd b. Thabit copied them out in a single volume, his work being assisted by a committee set up for the purpose. In the event of difference of opinion about the pronunciation of any particular word, the committee were instructed that the word should be written out according to the pronunciation of the tribe of Mudar as the Qur'an had been revealed in that dialect.

During 'Umar's caliphate, in addition to the improvements to the Mosques of Makka and Madina, at least one thousand mosques were constructed. The services of mu'adhdhins to assemble, and imams to lead, the congregational prayers, were paid for by the state. The mosques were spread throughout the empire, wherever the Muslims settled, and schools were attached to them for the teaching of the Qur'an. Another innovation of 'Umar's was that the teachers were paid: in Madina, the rate was fifteen dirhams a month. 'Umar was concerned that the text should be correctly vocalized and chose and instructed teachers accordingly. Besides the Qur'an, he made compulsory the study of some Arabic literature (in particular, morally instructive poetry and proverbs), intending thereby that students should themselves learn to distinguish right from wrong vowels. Provincial governors were empowered to grant special stipends to those who were striving to learn the Qur'an by heart. 'Umar commended learning five suras above others—al-Baqara, al-Nisa', al-Ma'ida, al-Hajj, and al-Nur—because they contained many of the explicit injunctions or laws that all Muslims needed to know, especially if they exercised authority over others. 'Umar asked to be notified of the names of the *huffaz* (singular *hafiz*), that is those who had the whole Qur'an by heart, in case he needed to post them where teachers were in short supply. The numbers of such men grew rapidly— Sa'd b. Abi Waqqas wrote to the Caliph that there were 300 *huffaz* under his command alone. As the encouragement of a state stipend was no longer necessary, 'Umar withdrew it.

Sayings of the Prophet (the Hadith)

During the Prophet's lifetime, there was some writing down but no formal science or *'ilm* associated with the *ahadith* (literally, sayings; singular, *hadith*; collectively 'the Hadith'). While he was there to clarify any point of doubt, there was hardly a need for such a science. But as different Companions went to him with their queries on different occasions, no one Companion knew all of his responses to all of those queries. To some extent during Abu Bakr's caliphate, much more so during 'Umar's which was crowded with events, new circumstances arose and there was general consensus that they be dealt with in the light of the Prophet's teachings. 'Umar's practice was to announce any new problem in the Assembly and ask the Companions what *ahadith* they knew that had a bearing on the subject. A great diversity of questions were settled in this way—for example, the detail of the form of funeral prayers, and whether *jizya* could be levied on the Magians as it could on the People of the Book.

'Umar himself was reluctant to report *ahadith*, and he urged others to be restrained also. In this policy he followed closely the example of Abu Bakr, who had at one time written down 500 *ahadith* that he later burnt, fearing that the persons on whose authority he had written them might have erred to some degree. 'Umar went further. He not only demanded assurances of a narrator's trustworthiness but also his power of understanding. Under 'Umar's influence, the people grasped, rather better than was the case in later times, the gravity of attributing words to the Prophet. It is reported (Ibn Sa'd, 3:157) of 'Abdullah b. Mas'ud, in some respects a pupil of 'Umar, that he would change colour when he narrated *ahadith* and frequently add, 'The Messenger of God said this word or something very like it or nearly so.' Imam Shu'bi relates that he spent some two years with the Caliph's son 'Abdullah, and in that period heard from him only one *hadith* (Darimi, 1:84). Similarly, Sa'ib b. Yazid says that he accompanied Sa'd b. Abi Waqqas on a journey from Makka to Madina but heard not a single *hadith* from him.

It would be an exaggeration, indeed an error of fact, to say that 'Umar impeded public knowledge of the Hadith. Rather, he was properly concerned that the centrality and priority of the Qur'an should not be undermined, and that the Muslims should not be led into error (or needless, petty complications) by mis-reported or misconstrued *ahadith*. Therefore, he would not permit people to report the Prophet's sayings unless he was confident of both their authenticity and of the competence of the persons reporting to understand their meaning and relevance. Once assured in both those respects, 'Umar urged the teaching of Hadith and adherence to what was commanded or commended therein. He sent such esteemed Companions as 'Abdullah b. Mas'ud, 'Ubada b. al-Samit and Abu Darda' to the provinces to teach the Hadith, instructing governors not to exceed or evade what was in their reports. Also, he had reliable transcripts of certain *ahadith* sent to district officers so that they would become widely known.

Understanding the guidance as Law or fiqh

Islamic Law could not have evolved without exertion of conscience and reason by the Muslims. The legal injunctions in the Qur'an do not cover all eventualities when an injunction is needed; some are general and their applicability in particular circumstances needs reasoning; others are particular and the general legal principle thus exemplified needs reasoning out. The Muslims' first recourse after the Qur'an was, on the authority of the Qur'an, to the Prophet's teaching, whether expressed in words or deeds or by explicit approval of a decision or action or by tacit approval, that is, by non-rejection. The Prophet questioned Mu'adh b. Jabal, whom he appointed as governor to the people of Yemen, about how he would adjudicate cases that came before him, and approved Mu'adh's answer—that he would judge by Qur'an and Sunna, and where he could not, he would exercise his own judgement (*ijtihad*). Abu Bakr, faced with cases of this kind, put them to an assembly of senior Companions, and decided according to the consensus of opinion among them or *ijma'*. The practice of analogical deduction or *qiyas*, as a third procedure for deciding difficult issues, was introduced by 'Umar. This is clear from his written instruction to judges, cited earlier (p. 102). The first formal, explicit statement of the principles of Islamic jurisprudence (*usul al-fiqh*) was written by Imam Shafi'i. However, schools of law, following the verdicts and patterns of argument of Imams Malik and Abu Hanifa, were by then well established. The reason for the differences between Maliki and Hanafi, and between them and the Shafi'i school, arose less from differences in the principles of *fiqh* than from differences in the particular *ahadith* available to them, and the difference in their attitudes to the Hadith in general. It would be digressive to go into the detail of the matter. What is relevant here is to explain 'Umar's attitude to the Hadith, which proved so important in the earliest period of Islamic Law.

First, 'Umar did not, as it were, go looking for *ahadith* until there was a need to do so. When a legal question had to be decided for which the authority of the Sunna was desirable, 'Umar asked in the Assembly for people with relevant knowledge to bring it forward. Otherwise, 'Umar did not seek to introduce intricacies and complications where there were none. His general attitude was to rely, whenever possible, upon good sense and sincere intention combined with a sound conscience. It may be illustrated by the following incidents: On a journey in the company of 'Amr b. al-'As and others, 'Umar alighted by a pond. 'Amr asked some people if wild animals drank from the pond. 'Umar asked them not to answer the question (Maliki, 51). Similarly, on an occasion in Ramadan, owing to clouds, people believed the sun to have set and accordingly broke their fast, 'Umar among them. A little later the sun appeared again and the people were distraught. 'Umar said: 'It is not a serious matter. We did our best.'

In the first case, 'Umar's thinking exemplifies the principle that if a thing is evidently all right, there is little virtue in inquiring too deeply into it, and certainly no obligation to do so. The second exemplifies the principle of the primacy of intention in religious observances. The intention and the effort of observance together are weightier than minor ritual detail required in the observance; error or omission in such detail, if obviously unintended, does not necessarily invalidate an observance. 'Umar's desire not to burden the religion with difficulties, to steer the believers away from obsessiveness in their relationship with it, explains why he himself, and those who were most influenced by him, did not narrate the Hadith excessively.

Second, 'Umar distinguished among the *ahadith* between, on the one hand, those decisions and actions that have the authority of the Prophet as God's Messenger and therefore have, for all Muslims, the weight of explicit and permanent laws; and, on the other, those that relate to his personal preferences or to his judgements in response to circumstances by their nature transient, and that are, for all Muslims, the means to know and love his person, and to seek to emulate him, but are not laws as such. This distinction is not accepted by Imam Shafi'i: he insists, on the contrary, that the Prophet's words (if authentically reported) are binding as law even when they concern such matters as the disposition of forces on the battlefield, assessment of customs duties or land taxes, and so on. However, it appears, from incidents during the Prophet's lifetime and subsequently, that such a distinction was accepted. For example, on the treatment of prisoners after the battle of Badr, 'Umar differed in his judgement from the Prophet; when the Prophet expressed an intention to say the funeral prayers for 'Abdullah b. Ubayy, 'Umar asked: 'Would you say funeral prayers for [a hypocrite]?' (Bukhari, 2:252). On both occasions a Qur'anic revelation settled the matter. 'Umar also questioned the terms of the treaty of Hudaybiya; this time, the Qur'anic revelation showed that his reasoning had been naive. During the Tabuk expedition, the Prophet fixed a rate of one dinar per head for *jizya*; 'Umar levied different rates in different countries. The Prophet did not prescribe any specific penalty for drunkenness; 'Umar prescribed eighty lashes. Until, as Caliph, 'Umar forbade the practice, it was permissible to sell slave-women who bore children.

It is inconceivable that 'Umar could have acted as he did if it were not, at that time, accepted that some but not all the Prophet's actions and sayings are legally binding; the Companions would not, indeed should not, have tolerated his rule over them. If no such distinction is made, it means that all the Hadith are equally valid as law, regardless of whether the words or actions were intended as a command, whether they record a single act (and exceptional acts are often easier to remember and record), or a regular usage.

Third, 'Umar questioned the juristic value of a *hadith* reported by a single individual, not corroborated by others. It has been the opinion of many eminent jurists since 'Umar's time, notably Imam Shafi'i, that such a *hadith* can affect the legal meaning of a Qur'anic injunction, for example by making a general injunction particular or, conversely, a particular one general. If the matter in hand was not one of very great consequence, 'Umar did sometimes accept such *ahadith* as a basis to form a judgement. Otherwise, he required the reporter of the *hadith* to produce confirmation. For example, a verse of the Qur'an (65.6), referring to the waiting period before a divorce is finalized, commands the husbands with regard to their wives: 'Lodge them where you lodged before.' This right of lodging was understood (see, for example, 2.235) to imply a right of board as well. However, a Companion, Fatima b. Qays, reported to 'Umar that when her husband divorced her she went to the Prophet to ask if she had the right of board with lodging, and he had replied in the negative. 'Umar said: 'We cannot abandon the Book of God on the word of one of whom we do not know whether she remembers the *hadith* correctly or has forgotten it' (Muslim, 5:343; *trans.*, 2:772). In the context 'to remember correctly' must mean remembering, as well as the words spoken, the occasion and context of the *hadith* in relation to the Qur'anic verse.

Abu Musa Ash'ari once called on 'Umar and by way of seeking to get his attention greeted him three times with *as-salamu 'alaykum*, each time adding 'Abu Musa is here.' As 'Umar remained preoccupied and did not respond, Abu Musa left. When 'Umar had finished what he was doing, he asked after Abu Musa and had him called back. Abu Musa explained why he had left: 'I have heard the Prophet say: "Ask permission [to enter] three times; if you do not receive permission, depart."' 'Umar demanded corroboration for this report, adding that Abu Musa would be punished if there were none. Abu Musa took his case to the Companions; Abu Sa'id came to the Caliph and confirmed that the Prophet's saying had been correctly reported. Ubayy b. Ka'b then said to the Caliph: "Umar, do you want to persecute the Companions of God's Messenger?' 'Umar explained that he only desired confirmation of a *hadith* that had reached him. (The incident is recorded in Muslim, 17:359–60; *trans.*, 3:1178.) 'Umar's anxiety about Hadith reports was neither intended to cast doubt on the authority of the Hadith as a whole, nor to question the sincerity of the people who reported. Rather, the corroboration 'Umar sought contributed to establishing what was reported as a usage, a confirmed judgement, of the Prophet, not an isolated case. If he was stern in bringing certain individuals to question, it was because he grasped the gravity of the consequences of reports from those who (like Abu Musa) commanded great respect and influence.

'Umar's integrity and the sincerity of his motives on the subject of Hadith were doubted by no one. There are several reasons. He never tried to impose his own understanding of Qur'an and Sunna as law; he always proceeded after public consultation with other senior Companions. He allowed differences of opinion; under his leadership, differences among the Muslims did not lead to divisions. At no time did he act in defiance of the Law as generally known and understood, or compel others to do so, not even when his own judgement was flatly rejected. For example, he appears to have disapproved of Muslims marrying women from among the People of the Book. Many Muslims took Christian wives after the conquest of Iraq. 'Umar accordingly wrote to Hudhayfa b. al-Yaman expressing strong disapproval. In his reply Hudhayfa asked if the disapproval was a matter of Law or the Caliph's personal opinion. When 'Umar confirmed that it was his opinion, Hudhayfa wrote back that he was not then bound to follow it. Lastly, 'Umar valued and sought the authority of Hadith on questions of law that puzzled him, in particular: inheritance of the paternal grandfather, of one who has left no offspring or parents, and certain varieties of interest. Succession to the caliphate is also cited as a matter on which 'Umar wished the Prophet had left a clear directive. That question and inheritance of the paternal grandfather were still on his mind when he was on his deathbed (Ibn Kathir, 1:162).

'Umar's contribution to fiqh

Most experts on the subject count six men among the Prophet's Companions as the 'pillars' of fiqh, that is, the founders and chief supports of the science. They are: 'Umar, 'Ali, 'Abdullah b. Mas'ud, Ubayy b. Ka'b, Zayd b. Thabit and Abu Musa Ash'ari. Others add to this list Mu'adh b. Jabal and 'Abdullah b. 'Abbas. Of these men, Ibn Mas'ud and Ibn 'Abbas were very close to 'Umar and learnt from him; Zayd served him as a personal secretary for a long time; and with Abu Musa, 'Umar often discussed legal issues in written correspondence. The majority of these men therefore argued their judgements in the same manner as 'Umar, and their contribution to fiqh owes much to him.

'Umar's own legal dicta, as attributed by reliable authorities, number several thousands, of which about one thousand relate to matters of fundamental importance for the Law and the science of it. In all these matters, all four of the orthodox schools of the Law follow 'Umar closely. (For details, see Shah Wali-Allah, 2:84.) The Companions accepted, even if they did not agree, 'Umar's rulings. In some very few cases where the Companions differed, subsequent opinion has supported their judgement as more correct than the Caliph's: an example would be the details of the ritual purification necessary after sexual intercourse. On questions of wider significance for the cultural and political life of the Muslims, 'Umar's judgements and, more important, his reasoning, have been upheld by succeeding generations. To illustrate, we shall briefly go through his reasoning on the related questions of khums, fay', and the 'garden of Fadak'.

Khums or 'the Fifth' refers to the one-fifth of spoils of war reserved by decree of the Qur'an as belonging to 'God and the Messenger and to the near of kin, and the orphans and the poor and the wayfarers.' All controversy centred on the meaning of 'belong to the near of kin'. The decree in effect reserves an income for the state and indicates five ways of disbursing it: the head of state; his near of kin; and so on. The Prophet's practice was as follows: he did give from this Fifth to the Banu Hashim and Muttalib, not equal shares, nor shares corresponding to shares of inheritance, but according to need so that (Ibn al-Qayyim, 3:94) 'the single ones were married, the debtors had their debts cleared, and the poor received according to their needs.' The Prophet did not give from the Fifth anything to Banu Nawfal or 'Abd Shams, who were also understood as referents of the phrase 'near of kin'. 'Abdullah b. 'Abbas and 'Ali argued passionately that the Prophet's family had an absolute right to one-fifth of the Fifth. If this were a legally principled argument it would mean that where the Qur'an commands zakah and indicates eight ways of disbursing it, any zakah collected must be divided into eight equal shares and disbursed accordingly. In practice, of course, zakah is distributed in any one or more or all eight of the ways specified. And that is how the Prophet distributed the khums, that is, he varied distribution, within the ways specified, to meet the needs as he saw them. 'Umar, as head of state, followed the same practice. He recognized and maintained the right in the Fifth of the Banu Hashim and Muttalib, but would not recognize any absolute title to one-fifth of the Fifth, insisting on his right as head of state to vary the distribution according to need. 'Abdullah b. 'Abbas, who opposed 'Umar on this point, is quoted (Abu Yusuf, 20–1) as saying: "Umar b. al-Khattab offered us out of the Fifth marriage expenses of widows and payments of debts of those indebted, but we refused and contended that the whole one-fifth of the Fifth should be handed over to us, which 'Umar refused.' ('Ali, when he became Caliph, while continuing to maintain that it was their right, also did not give the Banu Hashim one-fifth of the Fifth.)

Fay' refers to conquered lands. Controversy arose because some people considered such lands as spoils of war. The distribution of spoils of war customary among the Arabs, one-fourth for the commander and the rest among the combatants, was modified by the Qur'anic verse just quoted. After the battle with the Banu Nadir (4/5 AH), the following verse of sura *al-Hashr* was revealed: 'Whatever lands fall to you from the people of the town, they belong to God and the Messenger, and the orphans and the needy and the wayfarer and the poor among the Emigrants who were driven from their homes, and for all those who come after.' By referring to this verse, 'Umar managed, in the face of much opposition and after long discussion in a large assembly, to persuade the Companions that the conquered lands in Iraq and Syria should not be divided up but held by the people as a whole for future generations. He asked by what right he could 'distribute them [the lands] among those who are present and deprive those who will come after?' (Abu Yusuf, 35). In so doing, he established the legal distinction between cash and movables acquired by conquest and lands so acquired. (Both this legal distinction and 'Umar's reasoning about the Fifth were disputed, and rejected, by Imam Shafi'i.)

The 'garden of Fadak' was a piece of land that came into the possession of the Prophet by treaty rather than by conquest; the Qur'an alludes to it (59.6). Some Companions maintained that this land was a personal property of the Prophet and therefore heritable. Other lands similarly acquired were used by the Prophet as a public trust, and this was known to everybody. But he used Fadak as a private estate, spending part of the income from it to meet his personal expenses and the greater part on general purposes of state. There was doubt in many people's minds about the legal status of Fadak. 'Umar clarified the doubt by explaining that the garden had functioned as a private estate of the head of state as head of state, not as a private individual. Therefore it passed to the next head of state, not to his relatives. 'Umar's speech on the subject is quoted in Bukhari (4:211):

The Prophet used to take from it [Fadak] the maintenance of his family for the year. The rest he kept to be spent as the property of God. This was the Prophet's practice as long as he lived . . . . When he died, Abu Bakr said 'I am the successor of God's Messenger.' So he took possession of the land and used it as the Prophet had . . . . Then Abu Bakr died. Now I am the successor and I have had the land in my possession [now] for two years, and have done with it as the Prophet and Abu Bakr did . . .

The Law on slaves

'Umar did everything within his power, permitted by Qur'an and Sunna, to suppress slavery and, where that was impossible, to mitigate its effects. One of his first measures on assuming office was to declare as a legal principle that no Arab can be a slave. The immediate effect was that all the Arabs taken prisoner during the apostasy wars and then, according to usage, enslaved, were emancipated.

The Caliph could not have imposed a similar decree with regard to non-Arab prisoners-of-war. Nevertheless, the weight of his known opinion on the matter had considerable effect. The conquered territories were vast and the inhabitants numbered several millions, but we find few instances of people being reduced to slavery. Agreements entered into with the towns in Syria, excepting only Qaysaria (Caesarea), prevented prisoners of war being made slaves. The same is true of the conquests in the east; indeed, a number of the later treaties in the Persian provinces explicitly state that the inhabitants could not be reduced to slavery.

It appears that the slavery 'Umar had to deal with resulted from the local decisions of individual commanders. When informed of such actions, he reversed them. At Manadhar, prisoners of war who had been enslaved were set free by decree of 'Umar, and then assessed for land taxes and *jizya*. In Egypt, the inhabitants of a number of villages who were not regular soldiers but who had nevertheless fought against the Muslims were, explicitly as a punishment, taken prisoner by 'Amr b. al-'As and then sold as slaves in different parts of the Arabian Peninsula. 'Umar had them gathered together, set free and sent back to their homes, together with a warning note to 'Amr that he had been wrong to enslave them.

The worst aspects of a slave's condition are despair of change in his status, the indignity of it, and the isolation from his own family. The first two of these evils were mitigated by command of the Qur'an and Sunna; the third by a command all of 'Umar's own but inspired by the clear intent of Qur'an and Sunna.

Freeing slaves is commended in the Qur'an as an act of goodness, and one accepted as expiation for certain sins. In addition, the Qur'an envisages the right of the slave to obtain freedom; addressing the believers, it says (24.33): 'If you see good in them, make an agreement with them.' The agreement (*mukataba*), whereby the slave purchases his freedom by instalments over a specified period, was regarded by many Muslims as voluntary. 'Umar insisted that it was obligatory if the slave desired it. Bukhari (3:442) records the case of a slave, Sirin, who approached his master, Musa b. Anas, for such an agreement which the latter refused. Sirin took his suit to the Caliph who upheld it, referred Musa b. Anas to the Qur'anic verse (24:33), and flogged him.

Emancipation from slavery is meaningful if the freed individual is free to enter fully into the rights and relationships available to others under the same laws. It is not meaningful if he remains a despised or lesser being. The Prophet taught that slaves should be treated as equals in their person, deserving of all the considerations the masters would wish for themselves. 'Umar followed this teaching. We have noted that state stipends were fixed without regard to whether an individual was a slave or a free man. The Caliph had his spies inform him of the way his officials dealt with slaves; any failure in courtesy, for example failure to ask after a slave who was ill, was reprimanded. 'Umar himself often invited slaves to dine with him and made a point of announcing in public: 'The curse of God be upon those who feel ashamed to eat with slaves.' He instructed army commanders that if a Muslim slave gave protection to any people, it must be honoured just as if it had been given by all the Muslims. To one commander, he wrote: 'A slave of the Muslims is one of the Muslims. The protection he gives is their protection and must be honoured' (Abu Yusuf, 205).

All historians and jurists agree that it was an innovation of 'Umar's that a slave-woman who gave birth could not then be sold, effectively ending her status as a slave. He also decreed that slaves closely related to each other could not be sold separately but must be kept together. He cited a Qur'anic injunction about not cutting off one's relations (47.22–3), and said that no cutting off of relations could be worse than for slaves. To be effective in changing attitudes as well as legal practices, these instructions had to be widely known. They were. A father posted by 'Umar to Syria while his son was dispatched to Kufa, wrote to the Caliph to ask why, when he disallowed the separation of slaves from their relatives, he had separated him from his son.

Generally speaking, therefore, the slaves in 'Umar's time were spared the worst effects of slavery. In consequence, many of them became great commanders or leaders in different branches of Islamic learning and culture. In this chapter on the Law, we may mention as examples: Ikrama, one of the great imams in Hadith scholarship, and Nafi' who was the teacher of Imam Malik, the founder of the earliest distinct school of Islamic Law.

The prevention of misguidance

The careful balance of 'Umar's policies with regard to the Hadith is an instance of his concern to protect the primacy of the Qur'an in these first years after the Prophet's death. His ability to demonstrate and inculcate respect for the authority of the Hadith while, at the same time, exercising intelligence and reasonableness in translating that authority into laws, saved the Muslims of that period from much confusion and complication in their worship and in the general conduct of their affairs. There were also other (in most respects, simpler) steps that 'Umar took for the same purpose.

Ever since his conversion to Islam, 'Umar had felt a strong aversion to idolatry and what might look like idolatry. He cautioned people on many occasions against the dangers of sliding back into such error. Standing in front of the Black Stone of the Ka'ba, he once declared loudly: 'I know that you are nothing but a stone and can neither do good nor harm.' That people could easily become confused on the point is indicated by the fact that many compilations of Hadith, in which this incident is reported, add: "Ali objected at once and proved that the Black Stone could do both good and harm, for it will bear witness about people on the Day of Judgement' (Ibn Jawzi, 122). The addition, as many critics have shown, is a fabrication.

At the crisis of Hudaybiya (see above), the Prophet had taken an oath of allegiance from his followers under a tree, which subsequently received mention in the Qur'an. People had started to look upon this tree as something sacred. 'Umar had it uprooted and destroyed. Similarly, 'Umar noticed on his return from *hajj* that the people were rushing to a mosque situated where the Prophet had once said prayers. He admonished them sternly, reminding them that the Jews and Christians had gone astray by worshipping the relics of their Prophets.

Alongside clarifying their beliefs and worship, 'Umar did as much as any head of state can do to eradicate the people's vices. The principal vices of the Arabs from their pagan days were excessive pride in birth and contempt for others, a weakness for derisive satire, drunkenness, and sexual licence.

In every case of honours or stipends in the gift of the state, the Caliph, as we have seen, abolished rights of birth and social position. In the conduct of battle, the ancient custom of raising tribal cries was forbidden. Officials of the state who did not attend to the needs of the poor and lowly, who inclined to haughtiness of manner in any way, were reprimanded and, on occasion, dismissed. In private conduct also, 'Umar required his fellow Muslims to practise the humility and equality their religion preached. Safwan b. Umayya once invited him to dinner with other notables but, after the dinner was laid, did not ask the servants to sit at the meal. 'Umar was enraged by this and exclaimed: 'Heaven deal with those who treat servants with contempt!' (Ibn Jawzi, 96).

Intoxicants and fornication were forbidden by the Qur'an. 'Umar increased the penalty for drunkenness from forty to eighty lashes. Licentiousness was evident in the public domain only in the ribald love poems that sometimes even named individual women and were circulated publicly to the extent that norms and attitudes were affected. 'Umar published a decree against the writing of such poems; the penalty for disobedience was flogging. Derisive satires were also done in verse in those days, and poets were paid to mock individuals, clans, and tribes. Failure to reply in kind was not understood as forbearance but as lack of self-respect. The satires thus provoked enmity and hatred and were often the prelude to bloodletting. In defence of public peace and order, 'Umar declared it a criminal offence to write such satires. He kept Hutayya, a very well-known and accomplished satirist, imprisoned in a cellar until he promised to write no more satires. The Prophet and his followers had been the object of satirical poems, paid for by the Quraysh in the hope of defeating the message of Islam by deriding the Messenger. After some time, the Prophet permitted the poet Hassan b. Thabit to respond to these satires. Hassan's verses against the Quraysh continued to circulate even after they had embraced Islam. As soon as he became Caliph, 'Umar ordered that these verses no longer be recited as they revived memories of rancour and enmity.

9

The Treatment of Non-Muslims

Documents of protection

The Muslims' treatment of the conquered peoples of the Roman and Persian empires did not follow the practice of the Romans and Persians with their subject peoples. It followed from, and extended, the practice of the Prophet as 'Umar understood it. To begin with, he entered into formal treaty with the non-Muslims, thus recognizing them as a political entity and an equal party to a legal agreement. The chroniclers recorded some of the treaty documents in full and others only briefly since the terms were very similar. The document written in Jerusalem in the presence and words of 'Umar was as follows:

This is the protection which the servant of God, 'Umar, the Commander of the Believers, has granted to the people of Ayliya. The protection is for their lives and properties, their churches and properties, their chapels and crosses, their sick and healthy, and for all their co-religionists. Their churches shall not be used for habitation, nor shall they be demolished, nor shall any injury be done to them or to their compounds, or to their crosses, nor shall their properties be harmed in any way. There shall be no compulsion on them in the matter of religion, nor shall any of them suffer any injury on account of religion. Jews shall not be made to dwell with them in Ayliya. The people of Ayliya undertake to pay *jizya* like the inhabitants of other cities and to turn out the Romans.

The life and property of the Roman who leaves the city shall be safe until he reaches a place of safety. But any Roman who makes his residence in Ayliya shall be safe [therein] and pay *jizya*. If any of the inhabitants of Ayliya wish to leave with the Romans and take their properties with them, they and their churches and crosses shall be safe until they reach their place of safety. Whatever is written herein is under the covenant of God and the responsibility of His Messenger, of the Caliphs and of the Believers, as long as they pay the *jizya* charged on them. Witnesses to this deed are Khalid b. Walid and 'Amr b. al-'As and 'Abd al-Rahman b. 'Awf and Mu'awiya b. Abi Sufyan. Written in 15 AH. (Tabari, 3:609; *trans.*, 12:191–2)

It is extraordinary that the Muslims who had fought the Romans were nevertheless willing to allow them to remain in the province, if they wished it, under the same terms as the local people. The clause continuing the exclusion of Jews from the city was a con-cession to the prejudices of the Christians of that time and place, not to any prejudice of the Muslims.

Realities of protection

The sources record many instances where the rights of non-Muslims were upheld under the law against Muslim offenders. With few exceptions, the Muslims discharged their responsibility to the non-Muslims to the letter. Indeed, in certain respects, they did better. Non-Muslims who were too poor to pay their taxes were exempted, rather than punished; the elderly, and the sick or disabled among them received a maintenance allowance from the state, as did Muslims in the same condition. This practice was established during the rule of Abu Bakr. After the first conquest of Hira, Khalid b. Walid had agreed terms which granted to the people that:

when a man becomes unfit to work because of old age or is visited by some calamity or misfortune or having been wealthy he becomes poor and an object of charity to his co-religionists, he will be exempted from the *jizya*, and he and his family will receive maintenance allowance from the public treasury while he resides in the Muslim territory. But if he goes to another territory, the Muslims will not be responsible for the maintenance of his family. (Abu Yusuf, 144)

'Umar strengthened this practice by basing it on the Qur'an. He interpreted the phrase 'the poor and the needy' (two categories of the rightful recipients of *zakah* funds) to mean, respectively, the Muslims and non-Muslims, thus making the welfare and dignity of the non-Muslims a religious obligation. The justice, respect, and courtesy maintained in relations with the non-Muslims made co-existence with them easy. It assured the stability of the conquests as no armed force could have done, and it was a major factor in inspiring the loyalty of the non-Muslims and in making Islam attractive to them. However, there were rights on both sides and it is only to be expected that, individually and collectively, the norm of mutual forbearance was sometimes challenged.

Allegations of mistreatment

In 'Arbsus, on the Syria–Asia Minor border, the citizens, who had accepted treaty terms with the Muslims, repeatedly broke these terms and communicated to the Romans across the border the dispositions and movements of Muslim troops. 'Umayr b. Sa'd, the governor responsible, informed the Caliph. 'Umar did not, as imperial powers before and since have done in similar situations, order the city razed or its inhabitants collectively punished. Instead, he ordered 'Umayr to take an inventory of the lands, properties, livestock, and other chattels of the citizens, and offer them double their value in exchange for quitting Muslim territory for any destination of their choice. They were to be given a respite of one year to change their ways or accept these terms of exile. After the year had passed and the citizens continued to assist the Romans as before, the order to exile them was carried out.

Such cases were extremely rare. The typical pattern, alike in the former Roman and the former Persian territories, was that the local inhabitants assisted the Muslims, during and after the campaigns. Yet, in spite of all the evidence to the contrary, some have accused 'Umar of unjust treatment of the *dhimmis*. Their accusation contains a number of specific charges: that 'Umar ordered the non-Muslims to wear particular clothes as a mark of humiliation;

that he forbade them to sell wine or swine flesh, to ring their bells, and to carry their crosses in public procession; that he forbade the Banu Taghlab (an Arab Christian tribe) to baptize their children; finally, that he expelled all Jews and Christians from the Arab Peninsula, thus forcing them to quit what had been for centuries their homeland. In each of these cases, as we shall see, some historians (and indeed jurists) writing many generations later omitted to take into account details of context and circumstance that the more careful authors did not neglect in their fuller presentations.

'Umar did indeed order the Persians to wear a particular style of dress. His intention was not to humiliate them thereby but to preserve the distinct characteristics of their dress and that of the Arabs. 'Umar's instruction to this effect contains the term *zunnar*, which some later jurists misunderstood as a thin cord to be worn around the waist. In fact, *zunnar* simply meant any belt such as the Persians wore, and the word has the meaning 'belt', as does the Arabic *mantiqa*, and the term *kastij*, found instead of *zunnar* in some sources. When, centuries later, the court of Caliph Mansur adopted Persian dress, they adopted precisely those clothes specified in 'Umar's instruction, including the *zunnar*. The idea that the instruction was somehow intended to underline the Persians' subjection is a nonsense.

Forbidding the Christians to carry their crosses, ring church bells, and so on, would undoubtedly have been an unjust denial of the freedom of worship accorded to them by treaty. In fact, however, each of these measures was conditional; the error arises simply from recording the prohibition without the conditions under which it applied. On carrying the cross in public procession, the restriction written in the terms of the treaty was: 'They shall not carry the cross in Muslim habitations.' About swine: 'They shall not drive their pigs into Muslim quarters.' About ringing of bells: '[The Christians] may ring their church bells at any time except at times of Muslim prayers.' (See Abu Yusuf, 146.) These measures were obviously precautions against friction between the religious communities. They should be seen as means of achieving (rather than denying) freedom of worship, given the actual situation of two communities side by side, both wanting the same freedom.

Of the measure relating to the Banu Taghlab, the same is true, namely that it was conditional upon specific circumstances. A number of this tribe had embraced Islam and wanted protection against any tribal pressure to have their children baptized as Christians. It might be objected that 'Umar should have foreseen that such a ruling might be open to misinterpretation later on. But even if such a possibility had occurred to him, he would have reasoned that his present duty lay rather in preventing an actual injustice than a possible one in some hypothetical future situation. In short, 'Umar is not to be blamed for the historical ignorance of jurists who derived legal verdicts from incomplete and mangled reports of his instructions.

The expulsion of Jews and Christians from the Arabian Peninsula at 'Umar's command is a historical fact. The Prophet had expelled the Jewish tribes from Madina. His example has authority for all seriously practising Muslims, defining (at the least) the horizons of what is desirable in the conduct of their affairs. Yet, throughout the many centuries when the Muslims enjoyed political supremacy, there was no general policy of despising and persecuting the Jews. Rather, the Jews were well established as distinct, prosperous communities in many different regions of the Islamic world, and contributed greatly to its intellectual and commercial life. It follows that the expulsion of the Jews from Madina and then, under 'Umar, from the rest of the Peninsula, had its reasons not in some general prejudice, but in localized political necessities which were sufficiently well-known and understood for no general policy to be derived from that expulsion.

In Madina, the Jews had intrigued with the Quraysh against the Muslims, despite agreements not to do so. When the Quraysh came over to the Muslim side, the Jews' resentment of the growing success and unity of the Arabs as Muslims did not abate. Rather, they continued their intrigues against the Muslims with Arab tribes who had been formerly rivals of the Quraysh. The military campaign against the Jews concluded with the conquest of Khaybar, when they were expressly advised that, if their intrigues resumed, they would be expelled. That, evidently, is what happened. In public assembly, 'Umar listed a long catalogue of incidents, in one of which his son 'Abdullah had been wounded, and announced the decree expelling them.

Similarly, when the Christians of Najran, who dwelt in the Yemen region and who had lived peaceably enough with the Muslims, began to equip men and horses for war, 'Umar took a political decision to remove the danger their new mood represented. It will be remembered that the Christian tribes of the southern Peninsula had often been manipulated by Romans and Persians, competing for control of the trade routes that crossed their lands.

It remains only to add that these political decisions of 'Umar's were no dark 'secret of history' but publicly stated policy. The Jews were fully compensated for their lands and properties, as were the Christians. The order of expulsion contained, as well as provisions for their safe passage, a general order to assist them in their journey and a particular order to local authorities in Iraq or Syria to give the exiles cultivable lands once they had chosen their place of settlement (Baladhuri, *Futuh*, 78–9). As a precaution, a number of senior Companions were made to witness the document. Clearly, 'Umar did not regard these people as dangerous because of their being Jews or Christians; the danger lay only in where they lived and what they were doing from there.

10

The Man and his Achievements

His looks

'Umar was of imposing height and build, gaunt in the face with a brown complexion inclined to fair. His hair had receded from the front; he had a thick beard and long moustaches. His dress was extremely plain. He was usually seen in a single garment of coarse cloth which bore many patches, and an aged turban; he occasionally put on a sort of tall cap which Christian monks used to wear and which had come into fashion in Madina. He abhorred extravagance and finery but also disapproved excess in the direction of ragged or unkempt appearance.

His living

In the early days after the Hijra, while staying in Quba', 'Umar engaged in agriculture on a crop-sharing basis, but mostly he earned his living by commerce (Bukhari, 3:300). On the authority of traditions recorded in Bukhari (1:73–4) his excuse for not knowing certain *ahadith* was that his commercial preoccupations sometimes prevented him from being with the Prophet. The lands granted to him after Khaybar 'Umar dedicated as a *waqf* or charitable trust.

As Caliph, he had no time to earn his own living. He was

granted food and clothes of average standard for himself and family from the Treasury. Later, when the *Diwan* was established, he was allotted 5,000 dirhams annually, along with other veterans of Badr. When he moved into Madina proper, it was to a house near the Mosque that, on his death, was sold to clear his debts. It was for a long time honoured with the title, 'the House of Justice'.

His diet was plain in the extreme—typically, bread and olive oil—and guests to his home remarked upon it. His bread, if made of wheat, was of unsifted flour; sometimes there was vinegar as well as olive oil, and occasionally dates, milk, vegetables, and meat. During the year of famine, he ate only barley bread.

His manners

While capable of listening to the opinions and arguments of others, 'Umar was frank and decisive in speech. His severity of temper, of which people had been fearful before he became Caliph, did (as Abu Bakr had predicted) soften with the passage of time, but never to the point of indulging failings in his fellow Muslims. When he accepted the caliphate, 'Umar is reported to have prayed: 'Almighty God, I am harsh, make me mild; I am weak, give me strength. For the Arab is a sensitive-nosed camel and his rope has been placed in my hand, and surely I will keep him on the path, seeking the help of God' (Ibn Jawzi, 171).

As befitted the demands of his office, 'Umar was grave in bearing and speech but without pretension. He himself said that he could not make a wedding speech. However, there were rare occasions when warmth of feeling emerged in gestures or words that we might call cheerful. Ahnaf b. Qays, accompanied by others who had come to see 'Umar, found the Caliph running about with his garment tucked up. The Caliph called to them: 'Come and join the chase. A camel belonging to the Treasury has run away, and you know how many people share in the property.' Someone asked why he did not get a slave to recover the camel, and 'Umar said: 'Who is a greater slave than I?' When 'Umar saw for the first time 'Amr b. Ma'di Karab, a man of gigantic physique, a great wrestler and also fine poet, he is said to have exclaimed: 'My God! Is his Creator the same as mine?' 'Amr b. Ma'di and Tulayha b. Khalid, another giant, were famed as equal in fighting strength to a thousand horsemen each. Before the battle of Qadisiya, 'Umar sent them to the commander in the field, Sa'd b. Abi Waqqas, with a note to the effect that here was a reinforcement of two thousand cavalry.

His family life

Little is known of 'Umar's private life. Most historians agree that he was lacking in tenderness towards his wives and children, towards his wives especially. A tradition in Bukhari (7:489) records that when his wife answered him sharply for rebuking her, he said: 'So, you have come to that now!' Then she said that his own daughter (Hafsa) spoke in that way to her husband, the Prophet.

For some reason that is not known, 'Umar divorced his wife Jamila while their son, 'Asim, was still a baby. This was in the caliphate of Abu Bakr. 'Umar then moved from Quba' to settle in Madina. On passing Quba', he saw his son 'Asim playing in the courtyard of the Mosque, took him by the arm and put him on his riding animal. The boy's grandmother objected, and took her suit to Abu Bakr who upheld her claim. 'Umar did not object to the judgement (Malik, 588).

'Umar was deeply moved by the passing away of many of the great Companions who had been his friends and comrades, and whom he loved. Among his own family, he loved as much only his brother Zayd, after whose death in the battle of Yamama he grieved and wept intensely. He used to say: 'When the wind blows from the direction of Yamama, it brings me the fragrance of Zayd' (Ibn Sa'd, 3:378).

His relaxation

Although he did compose a little, 'Umar has no fame as a poet. But he is highly regarded as a critic of refined taste and judgement.

He knew all the major poets and learnt some of their poems by heart; his favourites were Nabigha, Imr al-Qays, and Zuhayr. On a military expedition, the Caliph once asked 'Abdullah b. 'Abbas to recite to him from the most poetical of the poets. 'Abdullah asked who that poet was, and 'Umar named Zuhayr, and explained his preference: 'He does not use rare words; his poems are free from complexity; and he treats only of subjects with which he is at home. When he eulogizes someone, he mentions only such virtues as the subject really possessed.' To illustrate, the Caliph quoted some lines whose meaning is: 'Qays b. Ghaylan has attained the summit of nobility; if anyone tries now to outdo him, he will only come to shame. If praise could give to a man immortality, you would never have died; but the adulations of men can never make one immortal' (Abu l-Faraj, 10:3754–5).

Affairs of state left 'Umar little time to enjoy poetry. But he evidently delighted in it. If he heard lines that struck a chord with him, he would say them over and over to himself. He was enraptured in this way by a couplet from 'Abda b. al-Tabib: 'Man seeks what he cannot attain. Life is wretchedness or fear or hope.' He recited the second line repeatedly. He admired only those poems that dignify human life and extol noble sentiments, and strongly urged his officers (military and civilian) to memorize select verses and poems. His instruction to Abu Musa Ash'ari was: 'Have the people learn poems, for they point the way to high morals, sound reasoning, and to the knowledge of genealogy.'

In some traditions, it is recorded that 'Abdullah b. 'Abbas recited poems to 'Umar the whole night until, as the time of prayer approached, the Caliph said: 'Now recite the Qur'an.' On a pilgrimage journey, a man was asked to sing the camel-driver's song but hesitated on account of 'Umar's being in the company. 'Umar did not object. So the man sang most of the night until the Caliph told him to stop as it was time to remember God. On a similar occasion, people asked 'Umar why he did not stop a camel-driver from singing. 'Umar said that such music was the camel-driver's provision for a journey (Shah Wali-Allah, 2:206; Abu l-Faraj, 10:3755).

His devotions

As Caliph and Imam, 'Umar led the pilgrims in the prayers and rites during the *hajj*, and served and attended on them. He went to Makka for the *hajj* every year without exception.

He said he valued the congregational prayers more than a whole night spent in devotions. But he did also spend the night in remembrance of God through *nafl* or supererogatory prayers. After that, he would wake his family for the obligatory dawn prayer with the Qur'anic phrase, 'and enjoin prayer upon your family' (20.132). It was his custom to recite in the dawn prayer from the longer suras (such as *Yusuf, al-Hajj, Yunus, al-Kahf, Hud*), but no more than 120 verses. If he had urgent work to attend to, and there was no fear of the time of a prayer passing away, he would finish the work. Also, he used to say that one should finish one's meals before turning to prayer.

It is unsurprising if, occasionally, the burden of his responsibilities overwhelmed his attention in prayer. What is remarkable is that he was unpretentious enough to acknowledge it. On one occasion he said: 'I prepare the armies while I am at prayers.' On another, that he had estimated the revenues for Bahrayn in that morning's prayers (Shah Wali-Allah, 2:90).

Abu Bakr b. Abi Shayba reports that two years before his death 'Umar began to fast continually, that is, one day after another, not alternate days. However, the same Abu Bakr also reports that when 'Umar heard of someone else fasting in that way he expressed strong disapproval. While not doubting his own capacity to balance active and contemplative life, 'Umar did not, it seems, like devotional practices carried to such an extreme that the worshipper retreats from his responsibilities in the world or becomes ineffective. It is certain that he did not regard dedication to the outward forms of worship as, on its own, a sufficient indicator of qualification for authority. He said: 'Don't judge a man by his prayers and fasting. Look instead to his wisdom and sincerity' (Shah Wali-Allah, 2:197).

'Umar was perfectly convinced of the truth of Islam as God's Will for mankind, revealed and complete, of the reality of God and of the Day of Judgement. But both his belief and his practice were positive. He showed no sign of that sort of obsessiveness which rests belief in religion upon its difference from the religion of others and therefore cannot be at ease with their difference, and may then degenerate into petty rancour and prejudice. When, in spite of his exhortations, a Christian servant in his own household did not embrace Islam, he simply quoted 'There is no compulsion in religion' (2.256), and left it at that. He was not troubled (as others have been since) about washing before prayer with water brought to him by a Christian woman. He did not think Muslims were exempt from the duties of exchanging hospitality with Jews or Christians. He never doubted that he carried a responsibility for the well-being of his non-Muslim subjects as well as his Muslim ones: he was concerned about them even on his deathbed. This inclusiveness and generosity of temperament derive from the guidance of Qur'an and Sunna, understood and practised positively rather than negatively, with a clear grasp of the Transcendence of God and the need to achieve contentment with His Will.

'Umar's fear of God was sharp and constant. Bukhari records this conversation between the Caliph and Abu Musa Ash'ari narrated by the latter's son from the Caliph's son:

'Abdullah bin 'Umar said to me, 'Do you know what my father said to your father once?' I said, 'No.' He said, 'My father said to your father, "O Abu Musa, will it please you that we will be rewarded for our conversion to Islam with Allah's Apostle and our migration with him, and our jihad with him and all our good deeds which we did, with him, and that all the deeds we did after his death will be disregarded whether good or bad?" Your father (i.e. Abu Musa) said, "No, by Allah, we took part in jihad after Allah's Apostle, prayed and did plenty of good deeds, and many people have embraced Islam at our hands, and no doubt, we expect rewards from Allah for these good deeds." On that my father (i.e. 'Umar) said, "As for myself, by Him in Whose Hand 'Umar's soul is, I wish that the deeds done by us at the time of the Prophet remain rewardable while whatsoever we did after the death of the Prophet be enough to save us from Punishment in that good deeds compensate for the bad ones.'" On that I said (to Ibn 'Umar), 'By Allah, your father was better than my father!' (Bukhari, 5:174)

His achievement

Great men are remembered and honoured in history for outstanding achievement in some particular field of endeavour. Thus, we remember Alexander for his military genius, and Aristotle, his teacher, for his greatness as a thinker. But Alexander's name is stained by his contempt for human life, for much as he achieved by brilliant initiatives and tactics, he achieved more by terrorizing the peoples he conquered. He was, like his teacher, a cultural bigot. Caesar and Augustus, both great commanders and organizers, laboured for the glory of only their nation and only inasmuch as they identified that glory with their own names; both were masters of political intrigue and utterly cynical in their pursuit of power. We do not study the works of Alexander or Aristotle, Caesar or Augustus, in the hope of finding examples for the conduct of our own lives. Conversely, there have been saintly individuals of the noblest moral conduct and profound spiritual insight, but their works offer little of direct value to the management of our collective affairs. Indeed, their teachings sometimes inspire the feeling that preoccupation in such affairs, necessary as they are, must be (more or less) renounced if we are to progress morally and spiritually.

'Umar attained excellence in several fields—in government and administration, in statesmanship and political craft, in the management of armies and conquests, in Qur'anic scholarship and exegesis, in the Law and the principles of its formulation, and in devotion and servanthood to God. It is difficult to measure, and therefore to state succinctly, the scale of 'Umar's achievements. Consider the condition of the Arabs at the beginning of his caliphate: the extent of the territory they ruled and the stability of that rule; the level of organization in their civil or military affairs; the degree of cohesion within or between their different tribes; above all, the quality of their understanding of what to do with the guidance of Qur'an and Sunna. Then, consider that, ten years later: they governed an empire extending from Egypt in the west through Arabia and Syria to Asia Minor, and eastwards through all the former dominions of the Persians to the borders of India; that their rule over this vast territory was stable, secured from internal or external threat, with their armies poised for further expansion; that these conquered lands were divided into provinces and districts answerable to a central government that organized and collected taxes and customs duties, funded courts of justice, public works, defence and policing, institutions for public worship and education, and the founding of new cities. Overwhelming as this comparison is, the most striking aspect of it has not yet been stated, namely that the Arabs now clearly recognized their new, growing power as issuing from and for Islam; in these ten years, they established patterns of initiative to deal with the legal, religious, and administrative culture of the peoples they conquered—whether they amended and adopted, or annulled and replaced, the objective of their effort with them was to establish the rule of Islam.

It is the genius of 'Umar that he understood what 'rule of Islam' ought to mean in practice, and was able to persuade others. It is impossible to imagine the consequences for the history of Islam if 'Umar had not persuaded Abu Bakr that the Qur'an should be assembled and written out in a single volume; if he had not persuaded the Companions to exercise restraint in the reporting of Hadith until the primacy of the Qur'an had become fully established in the intellectual reflexes of all Muslims; if he had not encouraged the idea that the Magians could be assimilated to Islamic rule on the same terms as the People of the Book; if he had not succeeded in saving the lands and resources of the conquered peoples for, as he interpreted the Qur'anic phrase, the Muslims of the future. It is owing to these and other initiatives of 'Umar that Islamic civilization penetrated steadily to all the people of the empire and, despite the disrepair and disfunction into which it has fallen in recent centuries, remains a permanent feature of the region. The civilization of Greeks or Hellenes, Romans or Persians, through the centuries that they governed the same region, remained always a property of the governing elite, the conquering race and the few who learnt their language and communicated their demands to the rest. Therefore, when the rule of Islam came, with its more inclusive ideals, those civilizations were absorbed into it and transformed—and not the other way about.

Many great, very able and dedicated men served with 'Umar— as military commanders, administrators, scholars of Qur'an and Hadith, judges and jurists. But it was he who picked out and directed their talents, prevented disunity among them and, for as long as he was Caliph, secured the many against the dangerous ambitions of a few. His guiding hand was the decisive factor in securing the progress of the cause they all believed in. The flow of military conquests did not cease when Khalid was deposed; administration did not collapse when Sa'd b. Abi Waqqas was dismissed, nor indeed when any number of officials were transferred from one post or district to another. If 'Umar was, in modern jargon, an 'autocrat', he was one who consulted before he took decisions, who not only tolerated but encouraged and enabled criticism of himself and his officers, who served not his own clan or nation or race but a universalist religion. If he was an 'emperor', he was one who never used an imperial guard to protect him from his subjects. He was feared for his justice and stern authority, not for tyranny or other capricious exercise of power.

'Umar's rule did not provoke intrigue against itself, because 'Umar himself did not conspire against anyone. His policies were always publicly stated, his own integrity always beyond question. The one shadow that fell across his relationship with other senior Companions was the disaffection of 'Ali. 'Ali did not give his oath of allegiance to Abu Bakr when the latter became Caliph. It was only six months later, when 'Ali's wife Fatima, the Prophet's daughter, passed away, that he agreed to give allegiance on condition that 'Umar be absent from the occasion. However, 'Ali's resentment with 'Umar for his part in the accession of Abu Bakr did not lead to a permanent estrangement. 'Umar recognized the wisdom and sincerity of 'Ali, confided in him, and nominated him as his deputy during his absences from Madina. Their reconciliation was sealed when 'Ali agreed to give Umm Kulthum, his and Fatima's daughter, in marriage to 'Umar, thereby connecting 'Umar with the Prophet's family.

To toughen his spirit, 'Umar's father had made him herd camels in the desert when he was a boy. He cannot possibly have dreamed then that one day he might be commanding a great empire. But when he came to exercise that responsibility, he never forgot the disciplining of his boyhood. The Commander of the Believers was often observed to travel without a tent, to make a pillow out of gravel and sleep on bare ground. He had learnt the disciplines of Islam at first hand from the Prophet himself and proved a perfect student. He achieved an extraordinary degree of self-command, a true humility not marred by the least trace of affectation. He once wrote to Abu Musa Ash'ari: 'People generally feel ill at ease with their rulers. I seek refuge with God from people holding grudges (against me), from preferring this world, from whims and caprices that become popular' (Ibn Jawzi, 129).

To this day, Muslims honour 'Umar as the epitome of the just ruler: insightful and decisive; clear in thought, speech, and deeds; stern, fair, pious, upright, persevering, disciplined, and humble. But the images of him that are most often rehearsed are rarely connected with the great affairs of state that he directed. They present him rather in the role of the people's anxious servant than their all-conquering ruler. They show him on the journey to Syria, unrecognized by his subjects and therefore able to get frank answers as to how well he is governing them; or doing his rounds of the city under cover of night; or watching over the tents of travellers to the city (in some traditions, accompanied by 'Abd al-Rahman b. 'Awf) and attending to their needs. It is perhaps fitting to close with one such incident, albeit one in which the Caliph is not incognito (Shah Wali-Allah, 2:196): a Bedouin importuned 'Umar in verse: 'O 'Umar, real joy is the joy of Paradise. Clothe my daughters and their mother. By God, you shall do it.' The Caliph asked what would happen if he did not. The Bedouin said: 'You will be questioned about me on the Day of Judgement. You will be taken aback [i.e. unable to make answer]. Then you will go either to heaven or hell.' The Caliph wept until his beard

was wet, and gave the man his own garment, having nothing else
with him to give. He wept because the certainty of the Bedouin's
faith moved him, or because the Bedouin's words pierced to his
own fear of the judgement of God. In either case, it is characteristic
of 'Umar that he did not waste the opportunity but acted promptly
and gave what he had. *Radi Allahu 'an-hu*: may God be pleased
with him.

Further Reading

Two of the sources frequently referred to by Shibli Numani for the narrative of the conquests are available in English translation: *Kitāb Futūḥ al-buldān* of Baladhuri translated by Philip K. Hitti as *The Origins of the Islamic State* (New York: Columbia University Press, 1916), vol. i, pp. 165–352, 387–494; and the relevant volumes of the monumental history of Tabari, published by the State University of New York Press, Albany, which are xi (1993), xii (1992), xiii (1989), and xiv (1994). (The critical notes to vol. xi by K.Y. Blankinship discuss and concisely demonstrate the hurdles that modern scholarship faces in dealing with the materials for this period.) Most Western scholars, finding the inconsistencies in the early histories of the conquests difficult to disentangle, have read them rather sceptically. They have been likewise sceptical of the early accounts of the administrative reforms during 'Umar's rule, even the institution of the *Diwan*, preferring to believe that these were later measures 'back-dated' to secure moral authority for them. This scepticism leaves the scale and permanence of the conquests unexplained. The problem of how to understand the transformation of semi-nomadic raiders into settled empire-builders is illustrated in a popular book by the Italian Orientalist Francesco Gabrieli, *Muhammad and the Conquests of Islam* (London: World University Library, 1968). Gabrieli (pp. 103–16) suggests a mix of motives: primarily, 'uncontrollable religious fervour' and 'the

irresistible goad of famine'; secondarily, a vague feeling in the conquerors' minds that they were 'the bearers of a new history, the
champions of a new race' and at the same time 'the propagators
of a new rule of life, a new faith' (p. 115). Among other historical
surveys from a 'secular' perspective are: William Muir, *Annals of
the Early Caliphate* AD *632–680* (Amsterdam Oriental Press, 1968;
pp. 66–285), and volume i (for the years 632–40) of Edmond
Rabbath, *La Conquête arabe sous les quatre premiers califes* (Beirut:
Publications de l'Université Libanaise, 1985). The most readable
narrative is by J. B. Glubb, a former soldier who understands the
military geography from first-hand experience. His *The Great Arab
Conquests* (London, 1963) provides helpful maps and analyses of
individual battles. A. J. Butler's scholarly and detailed *The Arab
Conquest of Egypt and the Last Thirty Years of Roman Dominion*
(Oxford, 1902) contains a very sympathetic portrayal of 'Amr ibn
al-'As.

Most Muslim scholars attribute the permanence of the conquests to the civilizing vigour of Islam and therefore tend to idealize
'Umar and the period of his rule. *Al-Aḥkām al-sulṭāniyyah* by
Mawardi translated by Asadullah Yate as *The Laws of Islamic Gov-
ernance* (London: Ta-Ha Publishers, 1996) abounds in references
to the practice of 'Umar as normative. The chapters on the first
four caliphs in the famous summary compilation *Ta'rīkh al-khulafā'*
by Jalāl al-Dīn al-Suyūṭī (d. 911/1505) have been translated by
Abussamad Clarke as *The History of the Khalifas Who Took the
Right Way* (London: Ta-Ha Publishers, 1995, pp. 105–49). A translation of the whole work also exists: *Ta'rīkh al-khulafā'* by Major
H. S. Jarrett (Calcutta, 1881, pp. 112–52). Self-consciously Muslim
reflections on 'Umar focus on individual incidents from his life
to exemplify his moral excellence, particularly as a ruler. Recent
works of this kind, even restricting choice to books in English,
are very numerous. Two examples must suffice: *The Pious Caliphs*
by Dr Majid Ali Khan (Safat, Kuwait: Islamic Book Publishers,
n.d., pp. 67–126) and *Hadrat 'Umar Farooq* by Professor Masud-
ul-Hasan (Lahore: Islamic Publications Ltd, 1982).

References

Abu l-Faraj: 'Alī b. al-Ḥusayn b. Muḥammad Abū l-Faraj al-Iṣbahānī (d. 356/967)
K. al-Aghānī Ed. Ibrāhīm al-Abyārī 10 vols. (Cairo, 1389/1969).
Abu Yusuf: Ya'qūb b. Ibrāhīm Abū Yūsuf (d. 181/798)
K. al-Kharāj (Cairo, 1352 AH).
'Ali al-Muttaqi: 'Alī al-Muttaqī b. Ḥusām al-Dīn al-Burhānpūrī (d. 975/1567)
Kanz al-'ummāl fī sunan al-aqwāl wa-l-af'āl. 2nd edn., 22 vols. (Hyderabad, 1364–95 AH).
Azdi: Muḥammad b. 'Abdullāh al-Azdī (d. 231/845)
Futūḥ al-Shām (Cairo, 1970).
Baladhuri: Aḥmad b. Yaḥyā b. Jābir al-Balādhurī (d. c.279/892)
Ansāb al-ashrāf, 7 vols. (Beirut, 1978–96).
Futūḥ al-buldān, ed. Ṣalāḥ al-Dīn al-Munajjid (Cairo, n.d.).
Bukhari: Muḥammad b. Ismā'īl al-Bukhārī (d. 256/870)
Ṣaḥīḥ al-Bukhārī (Arabic–English parallel text), revised edn., 9 vols. (Ankara, 1976).
Darimi: Abū Muḥammad 'Abdullāh b. 'Abd al-Raḥmān al-Dārimī (d. 255/869)
Sunan al-Dārimī (Dār Ihyā' al-Sunna al-Nabawiyya, n.p., n.d.)
Ibn al-Athir: 'Alī b. Muḥammad b. al-Athīr (d. 630/1233)
Usd al-ghāba fī ma'rifat al-ṣaḥāba, 5 vols. (Cairo, 1280 AH).
al-Kāmil fī l-ta'rīkh, 12 vols. (Beirut, 1965).
Ibn Hajar: Aḥmad b. 'Alī b. Ḥajar al-'Asqalānī (d. 852/1449)
Fatḥ al-bārī 13 vols. (Beirut, 1416/1989).

Ibn Hayyan: Muḥammad b. Khalaf b. Ḥayyān (d. 469/1076)
Akhbār al-quḍāt (Beirut, n.d.)

Ibn Hisham: Abū Muḥammad ʿAbd al-Malik b. Hishām (d. 218/833)
al-Sīrat al-nabawiyya, 4 vols. (Cairo, 1936).

Ibn al-Jawzi: Abū l-Faraj ʿAbd al-Raḥmān b. ʿAlī b. al-Jawzī (d. 597/1200)
Manāqib ʿUmar ibn al-Khaṭṭāb (Beirut, 1980).

Ibn Kathir: Abū l-Fidāʾ al-Ḥāfiẓ b. Kathīr al-Dimashqī (d. 774/13730)
Tafsīr al-Qurʾān al-ʿaẓīm, 2nd edn. (Beirut, 1419/1998).

Ibn al-Qayyim: Muḥammad b. Qayyim al-Jawziyya al-Dimashqī (d. 751/
1058)
Zād al-maʿād fī hady khayr al-ʿibād (Beirut, 1996).

Ibn Saʿd: Muḥammad b. Saʿd b. Manīʿ al-Baṣrī (d. 230/845)
al-Ṭabaqāt al-kubrā, 8 vols. (Beirut, 1985).

Jahiz: Abū ʿUthmān ʿAmr b. Baḥr al-Jāhiẓ (d. 255/868–9)
al-Bayān wa-l-tabyīn, ed. ʿAbd al-Salām Muḥammad Hārūn. Cairo,
1405/1985.

Jassas: Abū Bakr Aḥmad al-Jaṣṣaṣ al-Rāzī (d. 370/981)
Aḥkām al-Qurʾān (Lahore, 1400 AH).

Malik: Mālik b. Anas b. Abī ʿĀmir al-Aṣbaḥī (d. 179/796)
al-Muwaṭṭā (Cairo, n.d.)

Maqrizi: Abū l-ʿAbbās Aḥmad b. ʿAlī al-Maqrīzī (d. 845/1442)
*K. al-Mawāʾiẓ wa-l-iʿtibār bi-dhikr al-khiṭaṭ wa-l-āthār al-maʿrūf bi-
l-khiṭaṭ al-Maqrīziyya*, 2 vols. (Cairo, n.d.)

Mawardi: Abū l-Ḥasan ʿAlī b. Muḥammad al-Māwardī (d. 450/1058)
al-Aḥkām al-sulṭāniyya (Bonn, 1853).

Muslim: Abū l-Ḥusayn Muslim b. Ḥajjāj al-Qushayrī (d. 261/875)
Ṣaḥīḥ Muslim bi-sharḥ al-Nawawī, 9 vols. (Beirut, 1414/ 1994).
Ṣaḥīḥ Muslim, trans. and notes by ʿAbdul Ḥamīd Ṣiddīqī 4 vols. (Lahore,
1976).

Shah Wali-Allah: Shāh Walī Allāh al-Muḥaddith al-Dihlawī (d. 1176/
1762)
Izālat al-khafāʾ ʿan khilāfat al-khulafāʾ (Lahore, 1397/1976).

Shaybani: Muḥammad b. Ḥasan al-Shaybānī (d. 189/805)
al-Muwaṭṭa (Lucknow, n.d.).

Shirazi: Abū Isḥāq al-Shīrāzī (d. 476/1083)
Ṭabaqāt al-fuqahāʾ (Beirut, 1981).

Tabari: Abū Jaʿfar Muḥammad b. Jarīr al-Ṭabarī (d. 310/922)
Taʾrīkh al-rusul wa-l-mulūk, 7 vols. (Cairo, 1960–77).
The History of al-Ṭabarī vol. xii: The Battle of al-Qādisiyyah and the

Conquest of Syria and Palestine, trans. and notes by Yohann Friedmann (Albany, NY, 1992).

The History of al-Tabari, vol. *xiii: The Conquest of Iraq, Southwestern Persia, and Egypt*, trans. and notes by Gauthier H. A. Juynboll (Albany, NY, 1992).

Ya'qubi: Aḥmad b. Abī Ya'qūb Ja'far b. Wahb al-Ya'qūbī (d. 284/897) *Ta'rīkh al-Ya'qūbī* (Beirut, 1379/1960).

Index